THE INVISIBLE ASSASSIN

RON HASLAM

authorHOUSE®

AuthorHouse™
1663 Liberty Drive
Bloomington, IN 47403
www.authorhouse.com
Phone: 1-800-839-8640

Published by AuthorHouse   03/28/2013

ISBN: 978-1-4817-8842-7 (sc)
ISBN: 978-1-4817-8841-0 (hc)

CHAPTER ONE

T HE BANKER AND FINANCIER CLUTCHED at his throat, but it was a hopeless gesture, the piano wire that was wrapped around his neck was so tight that it bit deep into the flesh.

Trying desperately to force his fingers underneath the wire, the man tried a final plea for his life "name your price, any amount, in any currency, to any bank in the world, but please don't kill me I am begging you" he sobbed.

The pressure suddenly eased, he gulped air into his lungs, coughing so hard that he vomited down his $500 shirt.

A glass of water floated across the room of its own accord, seconds earlier the intended victim had watched as the large jug which sat on the bar, raised itself off the silver base to fill the glass, as if by magic.

"Do you believe me now" said the quiet voice.

"Yes I do" said the terrified man, massaging his throat "I never believed anyone could actually become invisible, but why did you select me to kill, I never considered myself as evil"?

"I saw your name in a financial report and read everything about you on the Internet, how you took millions from a pension fund that was enough".

"That was purely business, I'm afraid people sometimes get hurt financially, they are happy to make money, but then cry foul when they lose it.

Banking and finance is my chosen profession, I am good at it and know how to make money, but occasionally I also lose".

As he began to recover from the shock of the unexpected attack, the wealthy man's astute brain began to evaluate the opportunity that had presented itself, one that would never occur again.

He knew for certain that the invisible man would not harm him, if he was able to present him with an attractive proposition.

"Tell me invisible man, are you a killer, or would you like to be rich"?

"I become very angry when I read about the corruption that goes on in this world, someone like you stealing hundreds of millions from pension funds belonging to ordinary working people and simply getting away with it, somebody has to stop you".

"So you want to be an avenging angel" scoffed the banker.

"You would never understand in a million years, people like you never could" said the invisible man, "most ordinary working people do not envy you, they despise you, and are pleased when you are brought to justice".

He continued "everyone dreams of having enough money to live well and help their children, but not with money that has been stolen from their own kind, they prefer to sleep well at night, and wonder how you can".

"So is that all you are going to do with your life, kill people who are clever enough to make a lot more money than you ever could"?

"That is not true, I applaud people who work hard for their money and are clever enough to invent things that earn them millions, good luck to them I say, the people I am planning to remove from this life are crooked politicians, despots who ruin their country and impoverish the people who live in it, just so they can live a life of luxury".

He spoke slowly, but the banker could hear and feel the passion in his words as he continued

"Drug dealers who kill thousands of young children with the filth they sell, and the people who could stop them, take bribes of millions to turn a blind eye, those are the people I will use my new powers to bring to justice".

Plans were already forming clearly in the mind of the banker of ways that he could use the talents of this invisible man

"What did you do with your life before you became invisible"?

"I am not foolish enough to tell you anything Mister, I can imagine what contacts you have with your vast wealth of stolen money, I would be traced and put away very quickly, but I intend to make a few of your kind very sorry before that time comes rest assured of that" he said firmly.

"All I will tell you is that my grandfather was a coal miner who never enjoyed one day of retirement, he never tasted lobster, died coughing up blood, but he was as honest as the day is long".

After a short pause of silence the banker replied "regretfully that is how life was in those days, but you must admit that things are much better now, do you still intend to kill me"?

"You said you would give me whatever money I wanted, I am listening".

"I think anyone would have promised anything with a wire noose around their neck, seconds away from death".

"You are not trying to renege on your promise I hope".

The wealthy man knew he had to choose his words carefully.

"Absolutely not, I will give you the money as promised, you could have easily killed me, I am merely trying to ascertain what kind of a person you really are, you are more than just a killer I can see that, your ideas interest me, your invisibility gives you great power, and that interests me greatly".

"I would like some food and a hot drink, what about you"?

"Look mister, I did my homework before entering your house, I know who you are and what you do, I also know there is nobody here except you and me, your wife is away and there are no servants to be seen, three cars sit in the garage, a Ford saloon, a 4 x 4 and a Rolls, what do you have in mind, are you going to boil some eggs"?

The banker laughed at the assassins remark "hardly old boy, I can't even boil water, I don't need to, I hired a highly qualified chef.

My wife is in the south of France, probably with a boyfriend, and I have given the two servants the week end off, we are alone, you are correct".

Extracting a cigarette from a gold case, and lighting it with a matching lighter, he continued "I often use a restaurant in the town when I am alone, and cannot be bothered to go out, I phone and they deliver, the food is excellent and a good menu".

"Ok I will join you, but no tricks or I will kill you".

"Yes I remember" said the banker, ruefully rubbing his throat, "what do I call you by the way" "you can call me Jim" the intruder said.

"There are some menu's in that drawer, pass me one, and take one for yourself, choose whatever you like".

The delivery man rang the bell, Henry went to the front door, and Jim placed his forefinger to the back of his head as a reminder.

They ate the food in silence; the ticking of the impressive grandfather clock was the only noise to be heard in the mansion.

The owner drank a glass of expensive red wine; the intruder chose a can of cold beer.

"You may believe or not, but I am fascinated by your ideas of ridding the earth of bad men, but let us talk about the money I promised you in exchange for my life" said the immaculately dressed banker

"How much do you want"?

"To buy a small flat in Spain for my wife and me, enough money to travel every year, not like you would, a nice small hotel is fine.

I have a son and a daughter and would like to give a million to each; five million pounds would be more than enough".

"That can be arranged easily, but tell me more about your plans for others on your list, are you going to use their lives to extort money from them as you have me, if so you are no better than you accuse me of being".

"You misunderstand me, I want to use the gift I have been given to make the world a better place. I hope the fear of dying will make them change their ways, I really do not want to kill anyone. Of course I need money, but not for me, for my family, and it was you who offered it remember"?

"Let me tell you a few things that I have never told anyone else, do you want another beer by the way" said Henry, filling his glass with more wine.

"Are you trying to get me drunk so you can find and overpower me"?

"That is not what I have in mind, wait until I explain what plans I have of my own, do you want a beer or not"?

"If I misunderstood you I apologize, I would love another beer".

5

The shrill sound of the phone ringing interrupted the banker from what he was about to say "excuse me that will be my wife telling me a pack of lies".

"Yes of course, I understand you perfectly my dear, naturally you must stay longer, I will transfer more money to your account, and how much do you need? I don't have that much lying around in cash Ruth, you know me better than that, fifty thousand is all I can manage, sorry my precious, bye".

"Greedy cow" he exploded to his invisible audience "she expects me to pay for her damned boyfriends as well, she thinks I am stupid".

"Forgive me, as I was about to say I am rather tired of my life as it is at present, bored would be a better description, I have some ideas which may fit in with yours, we could form a team", "I am listening" said Jim.

"I also came from a poor background but I learned how to make money and sometimes it is necessary to be ruthless when you see an opportunity.

I am not proud of using a perfectly legal loophole to take the pension money; I have made many more millions legally by investing on the stock market, you hit a nerve and my conscience when you described me as a crook, I have decided to repay all the money to the old people".

"Goodness me, now you make me feel terrible, I nearly murdered you, how could I have been so wrong about you" said the invisible man.

"I think we both misunderstood each other and you didn't succeed, so let's forget it and discuss my ideas for a working relationship between us".

"First I must explain how difficult it can be to move large amounts of money around these days, the five million you asked for you can have, but I cannot simply transfer that kind of money to your bank account without raising questions from several places, mainly from the tax man.

What I suggest is some stocks and shares which I will buy for you, starting with small amounts and building gradually to your five million, and then I will show you how to make much more.

I know you do not want your identity to be known, but if we are going to be partners, I will need to know it, but only me, that I promise".

"That all sounds wonderful, but I am a little confused, what do you get out of this partnership".

"In business, do you know how many times we wish we were a fly on a wall, to know what is going on inside a board room, well you are my fly and we can make millions which you can give to the poor if you wish".

He went on, his eyes glowing with excitement "This will afford me all the excitement and challenge that I need in my life, did you not say you wanted to sort out some despots in Africa and some drug cartels, sounds very interesting and I like traveling also, count me in".

Feeling highly satisfied with the way he had steered the direction of the conversation, the banker said

"Are you hungry yet, I am starving as always, we can phone up again and order, I can hardly take you out to dinner in the Rolls Royce, wrapped in bandages like the invisible man" he smiled at his joke.

The second meal arrived by the same method as before, he paid the bill in cash, peeling off the notes and adding a generous tip.

"So wonderful to be filthy rich" said the invisible man to himself.

As if reading his thoughts, Henry remarked "You will be able to live like this soon". "Where do you live"?

"60 miles away" Jim replied. "Do you drive a car"? The banker asked.

"Not since I became invisible, why all the questions"?

"I will tell you when you have answered them all, now the last one; do you own the house you are living in"? "No we rent it".

"Perfect, this is what I have in mind.

I will register a business in mine, and the name of your wife, a detective agency I think, it cannot be in yours for obvious reasons" he smiled

"Second I will buy a house near here for you and your wife to live, put it in the name of our business, our meetings will be held there".

Rubbing his chin in deep thought, he continued "next we get you a face mask, some new clothes, a hat and some gloves, oh and dark glasses".

"You need to feel comfortable to be seen in public wearing them, and perhaps we will try some of those contact lenses which change the colour of your eyes".

"I presume you are wearing some kind of clothes, I cannot imagine you are naked" "Of course not, I am wearing a tracksuit and training shoes".

"Does your wife have a bank account"? "Yes she does" he replied.

"Good I will arrange a monthly salary payment to her of say 20,000 pounds. Last question, how did you become invisible, and when"?

"I truly have no idea; I woke up three days ago and could not see myself in the mirror when I went to shave".

"So the condition may only be temporary, we must move quickly".

"You have totally lost me Henry, why all the cloak and dagger, and setting up a business with an office".

The banker was pleased to hear him use his Christian name for the first time; he was now certain that his carefully thought out plans would work.

"It is the reverse of cloak and dagger Jim, it is to legalize everything in order for us to operate, and business cards will also be a good idea".

"But what is it that we are going to do exactly"?

"I told you before, but maybe you did not quite understand.

To go after the bad people that you are so set on bringing down, we will need money to fund everything, so we use the talent we both possess, you not being seen and mine for investing".

"What will you want me to do"? He asked.

"Exactly what I tell you Jim, you will stand in a board room with a tape recorder switched on, nothing more".

"What do I tell my wife"? "Tell her nothing except that she will be rich, it has worked well for me" he laughed.

"I will drive you home now, here is 20,000 pounds for expenses, give your wife half, that will make her happy, buy that mask and the other things.

I will look for a house tomorrow.

We also need to exchange phone numbers" said the banker financier.

"It has been one hell of a day" he said fingering the mark on his neck which was already feeling a little better.

CHAPTER TWO

THE BANKER SAT IN THE study, his favourite room in the six bed roomed detached house he had purchased several years ago.

He had lavished unlimited finance on this room, every conceivable piece of electronic equipment, useful to him in his world of financial dealings had been purchased, the best and most powerful computers that were available sat in their places, capable of giving answers to every question asked by persons with the necessary skills and knowledge.

Henry had learned his trade thoroughly in one of the hardest schools in the world, the City of London, and he honed his skills every day.

Several telephones, of various colours and designs, sat on the large black leather desk which was the focal point of the room, a satellite telephone sat near its bright coloured relatives.

A substantial wall safe had been installed, hidden behind a large oil painting depicting a fox hunting scene, the scarlet jackets and white helmets of the hunters stood out vividly against the dark varnished oak wall.

Inside the safe stood hundreds of thousands of pounds in various currencies, share certificates, stocks and bonds, financial loan agreements between himself and manufacturing companies, some from countries in Africa of projects he had financed.

The books adorning the whole of one wall were not the leather bound first editions, generally favoured by the wealthy; his books were all related to his work, and only passion, the world of finance.

The safe also contained small items of jewelry, bought for his wife in the days when he had felt some kind of passion for her, but much of his wealth sat in safety deposit boxes in his main bank account in London, he also had several other bank accounts scattered throughout world.

The rare stamp collection, the hand picked, and extremely valuable collection of diamonds, the small bars of gold, the priceless Icons, and even a Russian Faberge egg which he had been fortunate enough to purchase in an auction, were securely locked away in the bank vaults.

The wealthy banker had many things on his mind; the altercation with the invisible intruder had stirred memories of things that he had not thought about in years.

He had not been born into the same poor life that Jim had described, the only child of two loving and doting parents, who had sacrificed many pleasures in order to ensure that their only son would have the best start in life possible.

Attending the best schools and University, he recalled the sheer joy on their faces when attending the presentation ceremony of his degree.

Sadly he was never able to repay his parents for the love and dedication that they had unselfishly lavished upon him, two months later; they were killed instantly when a large truck lost control, crushing their small car.

Tears ran down his face as he remembered.

He had then taken a job with a stockbroker in London, dedicating himself to learning all he possibly could about the world he loved.

Suddenly thinking about a promise he had recently made, he picked up the phone and dialed his banker, one of his few friends.

"Hi Colin, how are you"? The niceties over and both were anxious to get down to business. "What can I do for you Henry".

"What is the amount needed to clear up the deal which affected the pension fund of those old people"? "Just a moment I will check the files".

"As it stands now the value is one hundred and three million pounds, why do you ask"? "I have had a change of heart, it is the only deal that I am not proud of being involved in, I have done much better deals since, the capital from that one helped me to make more, and now I want to repay it".

"I gave you the amount as it stood without charges and interest being added"

"I am not giving money to those Leeches Colin, here is what I want you to do, contact the Attorney and make the offer of one o three mil, phone the Financial Times and tell them what I am doing, making sure of maximum publicity, the leeches can forego any charges, they have already had enough"

When it came to business, the two kept it short and sweet.

"Will do Henry, be in touch".

Next the banker thought about the woman he had married ten years ago, it was a sham of a marriage, she spent all her life, and a lot of his money running around the south of France with all the other rich, bored women.

"Time to get rid of her I think, hello is that Mr. Jones the private detective, I want you to follow my wife, she is sleeping with half of the French Riviera, I want all the evidence for a divorce, yes photo's, everything you can".

He pondered a little more, "Five million should get her out of my life forever, thank goodness I made her sign that pre nuptial before we were married, she can find another 'sugar daddy' to look after her needs".

"Now to the next item, and maybe the best of all, my invisible spy".

"Hello I am looking for a two bed roomed Bungalow with a garage in this area for an investment, no, I don't need a mortgage, it will be cash, no I have no property to sell, will you send one of your agents to me in the next two hours with the details and some photo's, yes I want a quick deal, empty would be perfect".

"No, I am afraid it has to be within the next two hours, otherwise I will have to phone another agent, I am a very busy man, good bye".

"They spend more time telling you why they cannot do something than it takes to actually do it, no wonder this country is in a mess" grumbled the banker, he could not tolerate inefficiency.

Next he phoned a shop which specialized in electronics "Hello, I want the best pocket tape recorder you have, yes I will take the German one, make it two and include two dozen of the longest lasting batteries you have, that will be fine, I will pay by credit card, can you dispatch today"?

Next he phoned his invisible spy "Good morning Jim are you still invisible,

Sorry, a bad joke but I think you will not be sorry with our relationship".

"Will you bring your wife here tomorrow, I have found a nice small house for you, no just leave the furniture if you wish, you can buy all new with the money I gave you, just put your personal things in the car and move in".

"No I do not mess about my friend, time means money to me, and by the way buy a copy of the Financial Times tomorrow, my name will be mentioned, and you are responsible, no I will not say anymore, buy the paper, see you tomorrow, bye".

He rang for his housemaid, "May I have lunch in the next half hour please Mildred, I think a chicken salad would be nice, did you enjoy your week-end, good I am glad, thank you, it was my pleasure".

"Before I forget, an old friend is moving in just down the road, he and his wife will arrive sometime tomorrow, you may meet them from time to time, don't be alarmed by his appearance, he was in a terrible accident, his face and hands are badly disfigured, he wears a face mask, gloves and sometimes dark glasses to hide them, he is very sensitive but a nice man".

He phoned his invisible partner "Jim a small package will arrive within the hour, get your wife to make sure she takes the delivery, it contains a dozen different coloured contact lenses, please try them and let me know what you think, did your wife buy the suit and hat for you, good"

"I'm glad you are relaxing, you will be fine, see you tomorrow, and by the way, my maid is called Mildred, I told her you had a bad accident to your face and hands, she is expecting you, so don't worry".

A knock sounded on the study door "come in Mildred, put it down there, I will eat it now, did you bring my wine, oh good I will take a glass please".

"I think I have completed all the jobs on my list, now to think about making some 'real' money" the banker remarked, attacking the delicious food, and sipping his favourite red wine.

Switching on his powerful desk computer he visited the web sites he knew so well, searching for the data he needed, stopping to make notes, he then checked the current state of all the world's stock markets.

Nodding his head and smiling at the information which appeared on the screen, grunting in satisfaction, he noted all the latest commodity prices, left his desk and took down a thick book from the library shelves.

Thumbing through the pages, he wrote names on a note pad, checked back to a special web site, and made further notes, then as if not believing what he had read, he checked the figures again, letting out a whistle, he muttered to himself "I cannot wait to unleash my invisible spy onto several organizations who are looking to grow by takeovers, if decisions are made at those board meetings, and I know what they are, I will be in the big league of investors in the world, and nothing can stop me".

The black phone rang, he answered at once, and believing he knew who it was, "Hi Colin, I thought it was you, what news"?

"The Attorneys were over the moon, and the old pensioners are so full of gratitude, they want to make you the President of their society, they have invited you to speak at their annual dinner next week, I have to let them know what your answer is".

Ignoring the invite for now, he asked "what about the interest and charges"?

"All gone away, just as you thought, they do not want any bad publicity from the Financial Times article". "Thanks Colin that is good news".

"Why are you thanking me sport, it is you who has to transfer one hundred and three million pounds"?

"If the deals I am working on now come off, it will be worth it for the publicity" said Henry.

"What answer will I give to the pensioners"?

"Give my apologies, say I will be out of the country" he laughed.

"It is just possible that I may be" he said to himself hanging up the phone, "but everything has to be kept secret in this game, even from you Colin".

CHAPTER THREE

THE BANKER HAD EARMARKED EIGHT possible take overs that he was interested in, and now he had to train Jim in the way that he wished him to operate.

Using the least noticeable of his three motor vehicles, the Ford, he drew into the drive of the small house he had just purchased, and rang the bell.

A nervous looking lady answered the door "You are Colleen I trust",

She nodded, "I am Henry, your new partner, and hopefully your friend".

"Come inside Henry, Jim is sat in the lounge waiting for you".

Anxious to establish a good relationship with the woman, the banker said

"I hope everything I did with your husband pleased you Colleen"?

"Indeed it has Henry" she hesitated over his name, wanting to call him sir, "the money was heaven sent, and this house is just what we wanted, how much is the rent by the way"?

"It is free my dear, paid for by the Company which we are directors of".

"Another thing, what will I have to do for the twenty thousand a month you are paying me"? She asked.

He gave her his most charming smile "just go shopping my dear, and allow Jim and myself to do our jobs, all will become clear to you, I promise".

"Hello Jim, nice to see you again, oh I forgot I cannot see you" he chuckled.

"That is where you are wrong Mr. Banker" said Jim stepping out from the bedroom, he was dressed in a pin striped suit, black shoes, white shirt, maroon tie, he wore a rubber mask of a pleasant face with bright blue eyes, a wide brimmed soft felt hat, and a pair of dark grey nylon gloves.

"You look good, better than the last time I saw you" said Henry delightedly.

"I will be happy to travel with you dressed like you are now" he added.

"Jim, I want a rehearsal, we travel to Littleton tomorrow for a Board meeting at 2 pm which I want you to attend, and all you have to do is a recording".

"This is the best tape recorder in the world, you will take it into the room where the directors hold their meeting, and all you have to do is wait until the meeting starts, then switch on this recorder which will tape everything that is spoken, you only switch off when the meeting has ended, not before, or you will miss the vote that they take, which is vital to me".

"What if I sneeze or break wind" he asked in alarm.

"Then it has be someone else, they cannot see you" he smiled

"Take off your suit and become invisible, put the recorder into your pocket and we will record this radio from everywhere in the room".

He came back into the room, Henry saw nothing, but heard Jim's voice from across the room "testing, testing" he shouted. "No Jim, just speak normally, recite a nursery rhyme". "I don't know any" he cried.

"After me" said the banker "Bah, bah, black sheep have you any wool".

"Sorry Henry I know that one, I am so nervous to not let you down".

"You will be fine Jim, just think of the money we are going to make".

The city of Littleton lay in the north of England, 200 miles from London, therefore the journey for them would be 150 miles, taking under 3 hours.

Henry decided to leave at 9 am, taking the Land Rover for comfort, and after a substantial breakfast cooked by the faithful Mildred, he pulled into the drive of his new associate, who called out "I am here Henry, open the door".

They drove together mainly in silence, each busy with their own thoughts.

The satellite navigator that the banker had set, took them into the centre of the city, he spotted a multi storey car park, which was a short walk from their destination. "I could do with a cup of coffee" said the invisible man.

"Afraid it will have to be out of a plastic cup" said the banker, entering a take a way establishment and returning with two cups.

"Stand behind this wall Jim, we don't need to scare the locals with a coffee cup floating through the air".

"That is the building, the board room is on the tenth floor, you can follow me into the lift, I will take you to the tenth floor, then it is up to you".

"Right Jim, there is the door, good luck, I will wait for you outside"

"He entered the meeting room, his mouth was dry, a huge table with seating for 20 people dominated the room, a chair stood at each end.

Suffering a small panic "which end will the chairman sit", he answered his own question "wait until the meeting starts you fool, then you will know".

Grinning at his stupidity, he saw that pencils and pads had been placed near every chair, along with an empty glass.

Jugs of water and more glasses sat on a table at the far end of the room, looking around to make sure the room was empty, he drank two glasses.

The door opened at 13.55, the board members filed inside, and took their seats, the chairman was the last to enter, and the meeting began.

Jim stood next to a window, near to the chairman, and switched on the tape recorder, checking three times that is was on, and running correctly.

The meeting ended 5 pm, the members filed out, leaving only the uninvited guest to switch off the recorder and head for the elevator.

"How did it go Jim, did you get all of it" said the banker, unable to contain his excitement. "Come on I'll buy you a pint and a pork pie, to hell with you being seen or not, we will find a quiet corner".

Henry listened to the tape recorded meeting and was ecstatic.

"It could not have been better news Jim, you were wonderful" he enthused.

Sat in his study the following day, he phoned his stock broker.

"John I want you to buy 20 million shares in xxxx buy them over a period, not all at once, as always". "Had a good tip have you" said the broker.

"Not really John, I like the look of the stock and I am taking a chance".

After two weeks, the takeover was announced, and the xxxx shares jumped by 4 pounds, 50 pence, Henry phoned the broker again "Morning John, will you sell 5 million xxxx shares at best please, and send the money to my overseas account", the following day the shares had dropped by 1 pound "John sell my remaining shares in xxxx please" said the delighted banker.

"A profit of 80 million, minus the fees, not bad for a start".

He phoned his invisible friend "Jim I have just sold some shares from your portfolio, and transferred two million pounds to your account.

The following week saw them travel to Morganton, the home of a large Insurance Company who were looking for expansion, but who were they looking to take over? Henry and Jim drove up the motorway to attend their board meeting, uninvited of course.

"Exactly the same as you did at Littleton Jim; I will take you to the floor of the board meeting, and you do the rest".

They encountered a problem at the elevator, only one of them was programmed to stop on the 25th floor, the floor of the meeting, a security measure they overheard.

Standing next to the invisible man in the ground floor entrance, he held his arm firmly. "Jim, remember nobody can see you, wait until someone enters that elevator which is only going to the 25th floor, get in, and ride with them, it will not matter if someone bumps into you if the lift is full, and if it isn't then you will be fine, don't worry".

"Off you go now, quickly" he said pushing him firmly.

Jim almost passed out with fear as he rode the elevator with only three others, reaching the correct floor, it stopped, and he saw a security guard taking the names of the members entering the board room.

Jim had recovered his composure, and stood waiting for the right moment to slip past the guard and into the room.

It was a much larger room than before, the huge table seated 60 members.

He switched on the tape recorder and made himself comfortable.

Henry was even happier when he listened to the tape; this takeover was much larger than the last.

This time Henry bought 30 million shares, and ended up with a profit of 158 million pounds "Now we are entering the big league" he told himself.

He phoned the invisible man again "I have just put 6 million pounds into your account, and I have sent a large amount to the taxman on your behalf".

"I told you that the 5 mill you wanted would end up higher".

Henry drove into the drive of Jim and Colleen in response to an urgent phone call from the agitated couple.

"Hello you two what is the problem" said the immaculately dressed banker.

"We would like to offer you a glass of your favourite red wine, with all the money you have made for us, we can afford it" said Colleen.

"Thank you very much; I will take a glass with you".

"The silence and nervous twitching of the two people was worrying for Henry who said "Please tell me what's wrong so I know what to do".

Jim spoke quietly "Colleen is afraid that what you have got me doing is illegal, she does not want to go to prison, and wishes me to stop now".

"Look I can understand how you feel, it is my fault really, I have never told you how the stock market works.

Stocks and shares are bought and sold, and you can just as easily lose all your money as well as make some.

The market can rise purely on rumours of one company taking over another, and it can also fall for the same reasons.

In some ways it is a game of chance, but for the ones who understand it, have the money to buy shares, and the courage to do so, you can make money, but again I stress, you can also lose it.

Some board members who know there is going to be a takeover may tell their friends, who will buy shares and make money.

That is illegal and called insider trading, but it is difficult to prove.

In our case it would be difficult to prove an invisible man learns about a takeover, and makes money, to me it is no different to guessing there is a takeover coming. All the large investors in the world receive tips from good sources I can assure you, that is how they make money, but understand this, nobody is stealing any money from anyone else like fraud, it is the buying and selling of stocks and shares, which is the way businesses get their funding from in order to expand, and create more jobs.

I hope I have explained it to you in a way that you understand.

I intend to do only two or three more deals, and then we will all have enough money to fund what we will have to spend to take down the crooks, that you told me about, I still want to join you in that".

"I'm not sure that is important to me anymore" said Jim, and Colleen nodded in agreement.

"That is your choice, but don't you want to take this chance to make sure your family are financially secure forever, work with me on a couple more deals, and I will make it happen for you".

Can we talk about it Henry, must admit we both enjoy being rich, it just depends how rich we feel we want to be.

I also want to do something about the evil people in the world, and being invisible could help".

The red phone rang on the banker's desk; he lit a cigarette and allowed it to ring six times before answering.

"Good morning Henry, this is Ralph speaking".

He put out the cigarette and took a deep breath, recognizing instantly the voice of one of the world's top financiers.

Trying to remain calm; he answered.

"Good morning to you Ralph, what can I do for you".

"You have been in the news lately old boy; I am hearing good things about you". "Such as what"? He asked. "Paying back 100 million was not small change, and I applaud what you did, good for all our images" he chuckled.

Henry said nothing, waiting for the caller to continue.

"You must have done some good deals to cover a loss like that", prompted the financier was probing for information.

"I have been lucky with a couple of deals lately Ralph".

"A bit more than lucky I would say, some dicky bird told me you made a pile on two deals, anything I can get involved with my friend".

"Not at the moment, but if there is, I will certainly call you".

"You do that old chap, and remember, I look after my friends".

"I certainly will Ralph, thanks for the call, take care now".

Well, well smiled the banker, "my fame is spreading if people like him call".

From his study window he saw a taxi arrive, his wife alighted, paid the driver, and walked to the front door carrying her luggage.

He opened the door of his study and greeted her.

"Thanks for the phone call my dear, so good to see you again at last".

"Sarcasm is the lowest form of wit, or so they say" she replied. "I am going to shower and change, and then we need to talk Henry" she added.

"A pleasure my dear, I agree".

They sat together in the dining room, finishing a superb meal, the banker said "let us retire to the lounge, we may as well talk in comfort".

He lit a cigarette and waited for his wife to begin.

"I want a divorce Henry".

"Oh dear is that supposed to shock me so much that I will cry" he said, an acid tone in his voice.

"Henry I want a frank and honest discussion on both our futures, I don't want sarcastic remarks, let's be civil with each other".

"I apologize Ruth, you are absolutely correct; on what grounds do you want a divorce"? "Oh I don't care; I will leave that up to you".

"How about adultery" he said quietly.

"Her face turned red with anger "What! Are you mad, I have never been unfaithful to you, not once in the ten years that we have been married, whatever gave you that idea"?

Taken aback by her anger, he was a little flustered and unsure.

"You spend so much time away, I just assumed" he stammered.

"You assumed I was having an affair with another man"?

"Yes I am afraid I did, what do you spend your time doing in the south of France if it is all so innocent"?

"I run an orphanage for unwanted children Henry, and have for two years".

"Why did you not tell me Ruth"?

"Henry you are so busy making money, would you have cared"?

"I was happy the first two years of our marriage, but the truth is you are married to the Stock Exchanges, all of them.

We never went out together, we had no friends, I wanted children but I was frightened to ask because you were always away, or stuck in your study, making deals".

"I am so sorry Ruth, all you have said is the truth, do you want the divorce".

"Yes I do Henry for both our sakes, I don't want any of your money".

"Tell me a little about your orphanage before I answer that.

I bought an old farmhouse with the money you kept sending me, the local people in the village were marvelous, they helped me renovate it for free, and are planning more buildings, we house 25 orphans at present but I would like to take more".

"Do you like living there, have you met a man, sorry to ask, that is your business" "I love living in France, I only speak French now, and yes there is someone else who is interested, but I have told him not before I am free".

"Ruth I have heard all I need to know, I want a divorce also, I have nobody else in my life like you, but our marriage is over.

I had intended to give you 5 million pounds as a divorce settlement, but after listening to you, I am changing it to 10 million, also you will naturally keep all your clothes, jewelry and your car".

"Thank you Henry that is very generous, and it will mean a lot to the orphanage, we will be able to operate free of debt".

They both visited their Attorney, and signed all the necessary papers for a quiet divorce, he transferred the money to her account, and they were free.

The private detective phoned "I am sorry sir I found no evidence of your wife's infidelity, the bill is high because I traveled to France and to", Henry interrupted him "It is fine Mr. Jones, I believe you, just send me the bill.

The phone rang again, it was his invisible friend "We have both decided that we will carry on with your plans until the end, you have been very good to us, but more importantly we both trust you".

"Thank you both for that" said a very happy and relieved financier.

CHAPTER FOUR

Humming a tune to himself, he drove his white Rolls Royce back from the Golf Club, where he had spent all morning chatting to members of his profession, namely bankers who were looking to finance projects.

They had swapped ideas, enjoyed a sumptuous lunch, and some fine wine, taking care to stay within the legal limits for driving.

I must take a holiday soon he thought, maybe a Safari in Africa is a good idea, that is something I have always wanted to do, he made a mental note to ask Colin if he would be interested in joining him.

Hearing the unmistakable siren of a police car, for a brief moment he thought they were going to stop him, he slowed the Rolls and pulled into the left lane, the police car hurtled past, giving him a wave of thanks.

"Life is pretty good just now" he continued to hum the tune.

Back in his familiar study, he began to think about the next plan he had in his mind involving his invaluable assistant.

Pouring over his notes, the Internet and various other sites that he subscribed to, he narrowed his next assignment down to two major possibilities, one in London, and a massive one in New York, which involved a huge Japanese Company, this one was too large for him he felt, he would hand this one to Ralph he decided, taking only a small slice for himself.

He knew that Ralph and every other competitor would already be planning to be involved in the huge one, but Henry smiled to himself "they do not have an invisible spy who can tape record board meetings".

He chose a large foreign company based in London, who were looking for acquisitions, there were all kinds of strong rumours in the financial press.

It was not difficult to learn when, and where, the next board meeting would be held, he scribbled notes, and consulted his data.

He did a search on another company, but decided he would not pursue.

Thinking about how he would get his invisible assistant to New York, and place him inside a board meeting, caused some consternation, he would put his mind to solving this problem, before he made an approach to Ralph.

"Colin what shows are playing in the west end this week, uh, uh, can you get tickets, I am buying, and dinner naturally, book a table for us please, I will be at your flat in 90 minutes, yes with the Rolls of course".

Driving down the motorway, the idea suddenly clicked and he knew exactly how he would get Jim to New York, but first, the next deal.

He phoned Jim "Be ready to travel to London, there is a board meeting for you to attend on Thursday, you will travel invisible, but pack your 'to be seen outfit' we will stay over one night, I will take you out for dinner, yes Jim, I have booked a suite, you will have your own room with bathroom, I will pick you up at 9 am".

They drove down the motorway in the Land Rover with the radio switched on; Jim had selected the station, one that played classical music.

As usual he drove with satnav on, it took them to their parking spot, Henry had reserved a suite in a nearby hotel which they would check in later".

"That is the building on your left, the grey one, we have two hours to kill, I will take you for a coffee, then we can take a stroll if you wish".

They entered a coffee bar, went down the stairs, finding a table in a dark corner "perfect, do you want something to eat"?

Henry went to the counter and bought two coffees and two donuts.

"How are you feeling Jim", I'm fine", "got your tape recorder"?

"Christ I left it in the car, in my case".

"It's ok, drink your coffee, we have time to go back".

"A good job you reminded me Henry, I clean forgot". "No problem".

Normally Henry, who was a perfectionist, would have screamed and shouted at someone who forgot an important thing like the recorder, but Jim was doing a great job, he was always uptight before, best to keep him calm the banker thought, without him there would be no deal anyway.

After recovering the tape recorder, Henry checked the batteries, then he replaced them with fresh ones, just to make sure.

"The meeting is on the 17th floor Jim, I will ride with you".

Jim entered the plush meeting room which smelled of leather and wood polish, there were only 12 plush chairs around the table.

As the members walked to take their places one old member with a heavy limp accidentally lost his footing and walked straight into the invisible man who stopped dead in his tracks and froze, his breath came in gasps, and his heart was pounding. "So sorry" muttered the aged member, recovering his balance and proceeding to his allotted chair. "Phew that was too close for my nerves" said Jim to himself "I must be more careful in future".

The chairman entered the meeting, he was a very tall man, immaculately dressed in a black pinstripe suit, red dicky bow with a red carnation in his lapel, handing out a leather bound document to each member, in a loud, booming voice exclaimed "I now declare this meeting open".

It was the cue for Jim, who switched on the German made tape recorder.

The meeting was loud and stormy, one of the members in particular was very angry, and shouted at the chairman "I say we do not need this merger, we are doing fine as we are, and have done for 35 years".

"Then perhaps it is time for a change Horace, and we may do even better"

The chairman shouted back.

The arguments went on until the chairman said "Time to vote gentlemen, may I see a show of hands to accept this proposal, six vote for yes.

Now those against, Five votes, my vote as chairman is to accept, motion carried by seven votes to five, I declare this meeting closed.

"Goodness me that was a stormy meeting, it gave me a headache" said Jim, handing over the tape recorder to the financier.

"Well done Jim, you are a star, I will buy you a superb dinner and you can have whatever drinks you wish, are you interested in seeing a female stripper"? He asked, "I thought not, only joking". Said the banker

"I don't think you are you old buggar, you really want to go" said the invisible man to himself.

"I have booked you into the hotel so you will have to change in the toilet before signing in.

Jim came out of the toilet wearing the suit and his face mask, he looked much better than before, the eyes were brown, and not the startling blue of previous, nobody gave him a second glance as he joined his colleague.

Later, as they sat sipping brandy in the restaurant after a superb dinner,

"Have you noticed what little attention you are given, you look so natural dressed like that, you can live a normal life I think".

Raising his glass "All thanks to you Mr. Banker, you thought of everything".

"Incidentally Henry if you want to see a strip show, I will go with you, but do not ever tell Colleen, otherwise I will have nothing to pee out of".

"Let's go before you change your mind, I have not seen a naked lady in years, I have almost forgotten what they look like".

"Waiter bring me the bill please, and call a taxi".

The taxi wound its way through the garishly lit streets, the driver honking the horn, shouting obscenities at pedestrians and other motorists alike.

Later in the privacy of his study, he listened to the voices coming from the tape recorder, they were crystal clear "so much for quality products, you buy cheap, you buy twice" he purred. "So my invisible friend, another job well executed, we buy the shares now, and hope they will rise when the takeover comes, hopefully" he added with fingers crossed," you can never be sure".

The shares that he proposed to buy stood at 20 pounds, how much would they rise, and how many should he buy, the banker pondered.

He gambled they would rise 20% or 4 pounds, if he bought 20 million shares which would net 80 million, not enough he thought; he was looking to make 160 million, so he must risk more money.

He settled on 40 million shares, hoping to make just over 160 million.

He picked up the phone "Hello John, I want you to buy for me in the smallest parcels you can, 40 million shares, yes four zero million shares in ggggg, buy at best price, and charge to my account, thank you".

Now he had to wait, first to see if the takeover actually happened, and second, what happened to the price.

Henry was fortunate for the third time in a row, the takeover did take place, and the shares of ggggg rose, and stood at 24 pounds, 30 pence.

The financier whooped for joy and punched the air "did it again" he cried.

Calming himself down he phoned his broker in a voice, the slowest he could muster, almost sounding offhand "John I want you to sell 20 million ggggg shares at best and let me know after you have sold".

30 minutes later his phone rang "I sold your 20 million shares for an average price of 24 pounds, 58 pence. "Even better than I planned" he said.

The following day the stock market opened and ggggg had risen to 24 pounds 62 pence after only ten minutes. After one hour they stood at 24 pounds 66 pence. "Time to sell a few". "John sell 5 million ggggg at best".

The phone call came I sold your 5 million ggggg shares at 24 pounds, 69 pence. "Not dropping yet, try a few more". "John sell 5 million ggggg at best. The phone rang again "I sold 5 million ggggg shares at 24 pounds 68 pence. "I have made enough, don't be greedy" he told himself

"John sell 10 million ggggg shares at best". One hour later the broker phoned "Henry I sold 10 million ggggg shares at an average price of 24 pounds, 50 pence". "Thank you John that concludes my business for today".

"It has been my pleasure Henry, thank you for having me as your broker".

He made a profit of 183.45 million pounds, he was exhausted, he knew he had risked almost all of his fortune, if the deal had gone sour, he would have been close to bankruptcy.

The total profit that he had made since he had met his invisible partner stood at 421.45 million pounds.

The banker phoned Jim "You will be delighted to learn that your shares have made another eight million pounds, which I have just sent to your bank, and three million to the tax man to make him happy, this is a gift from me to you for your wonderful work.

"Thank you Henry, we owe you everything". "None sense my boy, we are good for each other, long may it continue, put your feet up for now".

The red phone rang "A little bird tells me that you have scooped another deal, when are you going to let me in on some of the action"?

"As a matter of fact I have a deal simmering which is over my head, I am going to hand it on to you Ralph, I want to talk to you about it, and I need something from you, but not over the phone, when can we meet"?

"My office tomorrow at 9 am" he said. "Go and jump in a puddle of water Ralph, your offices are 100 miles from me, and I don't have a helicopter or a private jet like you, find me a better time".

"Sorry I wasn't thinking, Wednesday at 12, I will give you for lunch, and I have the whole afternoon free to talk.

Will you be driving down in the nice white Rolls Royce of yours"?

"No it uses too much petrol, I will use the Ford sedan, see you Wednesday".

CHAPTER FIVE

RIVING A ROLLS ROYCE HAS to be one of the great pleasures of life thought the banker, he had opened the sun roof, it was a glorious summers day, the very best that England can produce, and when one does arrive there is no equal.

He could not afford to allow his concentration to slip for ten seconds with the man he was about to have lunch.

Ralph was one of the shrewdest operators in the world of finance, his brain was razor sharp and he would pick up on one small word said incorrectly, that was not for his ears, he was a master at finding a way to ferret out the truth during a casual conversation.

Enjoying the pleasant drive in his comfortable machine, Henry rehearsed what he would say to the mega rich financier, and what he must not say.

Arriving at the huge mansion which sat in 20 acres of ground, the tyres crunched on the drive made of loose stones and pebbles, and to prevent the tyres from hurling loose pebbles into any part of his precious car, he drove the Rolls at a walking pace, negotiating the horseshoe shaped drive, he drew up next to the magnificent house.

A butler opened the massive oak door, which was adorned with fittings of polished brass; he stood in the impressive entrance awaiting the visitor.

Glancing at his watch as he mounted the five stone steps, the time was 1157, "perfect timing" he congratulated himself.

"Good morning sir, Mr. Ralph is expecting you, will you follow me please".

Walking into the huge entrance hall which was constructed in light coloured stone, the décor was of Tudor design, swords, muskets, pikes and pistols adorned the walls and several oil paintings, all of them depicting scenes of ancient English battles, a suit of armour stood proudly in a corner.

A large man with immaculately groomed grey hair, wearing a maroon smoking jacket, his skin had that tanned look of the very rich, his smile wide and inviting, held out a huge hand in greeting.

"Welcome Henry, good to see you again, did you have a pleasant journey".

"Yes very nice Ralph, such a beautiful day, I must say your house is wonderful, the hall is exquisite, was the Tudor design your idea"?

"Thank you for your kind words, the hall was designed by me, I love English history, although I am not sure I would have survived long, wielding those fearsome weapons that they had in those days" he chortled.

Henry smiled back but said nothing; he had learned a long time ago there was a time to speak, and a time to just smile.

"I must say it was good of you to travel all this way, I hope we can have a fruitful meeting, beneficial to both of us of course" he give a warm smile "lunch will be served at 1 pm, would you like a glass of sherry before we have our lunch" he asked politely. "Yes please I think I will".

Henry sipped the dry sherry, which in truth was a little too dry for his taste.

"I must be very careful with Ralph, he is like a huge tiger ready to pounce, I can certainly see where his reputation comes from, he is a very imposing character who you think you know, but I think only very few will.

The butler knocked on the lounge door before entering "lunch is served" sir.

"Come along Henry let us eat" said the huge man, placing an arm around his shoulders and guiding him into the magnificent dining room capable of seating 30 guests. "All of this just to impress me, well I am impressed".

As you would expect, lunch was equal to that of any top French Restaurant, consisting of four courses. "Will you take a glass of white wine" offered the host, Henry smiled and nodded, holding out his glass.

"You don't say very much Henry, are you alright"?

"Ralph I am too busy admiring your beautiful house and your wonderful hospitality, I will have plenty to say later, I promise".

"I hope you will Henry, I am really looking forward to doing some business with you, but that is for later" he said smiling behind his large glass of white wine "for now, please enjoy the lunch".

Retiring to the host's magnificent study, Henry was pleased to see that it contained no better equipment than his own.

"Right fellow banker and financier" said the host, "time to discuss business".

"Ralph I have been tracking the potential merger, or takeover of bbbbb in the States, ie New York, with ccccc in Japan, as I am sure you have".

Ralph said nothing, but smiled. Henry continued "I now control a source that can deliver a tape recording of the board meeting which will take place".

"Good god man you are not serious" said the large man in astonishment.

"I am telling the truth Ralph I can deliver a tape recording of the board meeting, both if necessary, in New York and Tokyo".

"This is far too big for me Ralph, so I am handing it to you on a plate; I will only ask for a small slice of the action, say 100 million profits".

"What will you charge me for the tape recordings Henry"?

"Nothing Ralph, absolutely free of charge to a good friend, I hope".

"You can count on that my friend said the huge man, his brain whirling round, already counting the enormous profits from such a deal.

"Henry I will not insult your intelligence by asking you how you will obtain a tape recording of a confidential board meeting, but please assure me that you can deliver".

"Ralph I have just made good profits on three deals in six months, working on my own, and using the same source, I absolutely guarantee it".

"Now I need your advice and maybe some help".

"Just ask, you have it" replied the host.

"Soon I will have a need to travel abroad, could be to any destination, the commercial airlines are not suitable, and I am thinking about a private jet, I know that is how you travel, and I want to know the ins and outs, what will be the cost, where does one fly from etcetera".

"There are many advantages of owning or even using a private jet" he said.

First, you can travel where and when you want, without having to plan ahead". Second, it is much quicker, with less stress; you fly from a small airport, no queues, park your car and off you go".

"What about passport control and customs"?

"There is an official on duty, you have to let them know in advance where and when you are traveling to, but it works well, obviously if you try to bring unlawful goods in or out the country you will be nailed the same as on the normal commercial fights".

"Can I buy a share in an aircraft", my trips will only be occasionally".

"Henry I have the perfect solution for you, I own three small jets and hire them out, in your case it will be at a special rate, I will give you a phone number and you can discuss your needs with my man, he will arrange everything for you".

Raising his glass of brandy to his host he said "to the kind of friend and partner you need in business". "I will second that my friend" said Ralph, the two investors clinked their glasses in goodwill.

"Last thing before I go Ralph, the New York, Tokyo deal is yours, you let me know the date of the board meeting, or both, and I will do my part, thank you for your hospitality, and your help".

"I think we will have a good partnership" said Ralph," drive safely".

"Jim do you have a passport that is up to date"? "Yes I do Henry" learning not to ask too many questions when the banker was asking.

"You do, good man, when does it expire"?

"In eight years time, we traveled to Spain for a holiday two years ago so I got a European passport, am I going to need it"? He asked.

43

"Absolutely my friend" said the very relieved banker, "you and I, plus probably Colleen, will be traveling overseas in the near future, and we have to get you a face that matches the one in your passport".

"Gosh you really do think of everything Mr. Banker, no wonder you are so successful" said the invisible man in admiration.

"I try to Jim, thanks for the compliment".

Henry visited a maker of the rubber masks that were available in many shops; replica faces of many famous people were freely available.

Armed with a photograph of his invisible colleague, he approached the salesman "I need about four masks of this face, can you help".

"Do you only need four sir, it will be expensive, but we can do it".

"How much is expensive young man". "I will check with the boss, can you wait". Indicating in the affirmative, the banker walked round the showroom examining the sample faces on display "Technology is now incredible".

"It will cost 600 pounds" said the assistant, half expecting the customer to walk away, but Henry, hesitating for a few seconds, and pretending dismay at the price, while inwardly wanting to scream absolute joy, coolly said to the young assistant "That will be fine young man, when will they be ready".

Jim came out the bedroom wearing his new face mask, Colleen took one look at him and screamed with delight "I have got my Jim back, it is good to see you again my love, you look just as you did the last time that I saw you".

Admiring himself in the mirror, "do you know love, I think we will go out to a restaurant tonight for a change, I feel normal wearing this mask".

"Give me twenty minutes to get ready Jim, I am out of practice". She said.

He sat in the driving seat again, looked in the mirror, delighted to see his own face again; he waved to other cars as he drove them both to a restaurant.

The waiter arrived with the menu, and glanced at him normally as he took their order, and again when he brought the wine. Jim beamed at everyone who passed their table; they smiled back and bade him "good evening".

"Henry is a genius Colleen this mask has made such a difference, you saw for yourself, everybody treated me as normal, nobody stared".

"Could we now enjoy the food please" she smiled, as the waiter arrived.

When the couple arrived back at home, Jim could not wait to tell the banker.

"Henry you will not believe the difference the new mask has made to my confidence, it was like before I was invisible" The banker listened to him for ten minutes, repeating the evenings experiences, and said nothing, but thinking to himself "That is exactly what I wanted, my invisible assistant full of confidence, ready for the big challenge of New York, but first another takeover was about to happen here, and he wanted a piece of it.

"That is wonderful Jim; I am so glad the new mask was as good as you say".

CHAPTER SIX

THE BANKER HAD COMPLETED HIS meticulous investigations; a board meeting was due the following day, on the premises of a giant multinational construction company based south of London.

The company built every thing that could be imagined, and operated in most countries of the world.

Many of the larger companies listed on the stock exchanges of the world were continually looking to take over smaller companies for different reasons, but all of them related to finance.

"You can travel in your 'look see me' clothes if it makes you happy Jim, we will have to find a toilet for you to change in before we arrive at the construction company, oh I remember, there is a hotel quite near, you will be able to change there".

The journey was uneventful, if you disregard the number of strange looks and gestures which Jim attracted from other motorists, in response to the waves that he gave everybody; including a police car, the officer just grinned and waved back "Careful Jim, one of them will fancy you and start following us" laughed his companion.

"Oh hell sorry Henry, I did not think, I am so happy not feeling like a freak anymore, I got carried away".

"No problem" we will be there soon, there is the hotel.

On arriving at the gatehouse reception, they encountered a problem.

"Have you an appointment" asked the security guard, sat in the small office next to the entrance boom.

Henry thought quickly, he had been caught unawares "Err I would like to see someone in your computer department, I am a specialist in software programmes and I think some would be suitable for your organization, I did phone and I spoke to a Mr. Greening, Greenwich, I am sorry I have forgotten his name. "Have you a business card "asked the security guard "Yes here it is" said the banker, handing over the private detective card. "A private detective"? Said the guard raising his voice an octave.

"That is correct, I am also an expert in computers" he said turning away and smiling at the security guard manning the exit gate.

The guard consulted his alphabetical telephone list "There is a Mr. Greenbach in computers "Yes that's him" said the banker, feigning a look of relief. "Ok I will let you through said the guard, head for the Admin block, the Main Office". "Thanks very much" said the banker waving gaily as he drove through the raised boom. "Bloody hell" said a voice from the seat next to him "you could win an Oscar for acting, you were wonderful".

"Sit here Jim I will scout around" said the banker. "Hell knowing you, I would not be surprised if you got an invite to attend the board meeting".

The banker returned "it is on the fourth floor, we can use the lift or take the stairs, which do you prefer". "The stairs please I need to stretch my legs after the long drive and to get my concentration on the meeting".

"Good man, that's the spirit" said the investor.

The meeting room was bright and airy, all the windows were wide open, the blinds were all raised, Jim would soon find out why.

The 24 delegates took their seats, and out came the packets of cigarettes, cigars and pipe tobacco, it seemed that every one of them was a smoker.

The foul blue smoke billowed from every chair of the meeting, as each delegate puffed away happily on his choice of nicotine

Jim switched on the recorder and stood next to an open window, sucking in the fresh air, it was a very long meeting for him, as a non smoker.

"Hells bells you smell of tobacco said the banker" taking the tape recorder.

"Let's get out into the fresh air quickly, I feel ill". Said Jim.

Henry told him to walk around the grounds and gardens for an hour, he returned to the car to listen to the tape recording.

The voices could be heard clearly, one was louder than the rest, he gave his opinions in a gruff voice of north of England origin, using expletives which are commonly heard on a building site, but rarely in a board meeting.

"He must own a large amount of shares in the company" thought Henry.

The invisible man returned, feeling much refreshed

"We can go back to the hotel where you can change, and I will buy you a cold beer and large steak, what do you say"? "I say wonderful" replied Jim.

Sat alone in the comfortable study which was the focal point of his life, the investor brought up the stock market data on the screen of his computer, and read the current price of company fffff shares.

The screen indicated a buying price of 66 pounds, 16 pence per share.

Using his trusty calculator to determine how many he could comfortably buy without crippling himself with debt, should something go wrong, he decided that he would purchase 12 million shares, which was within his buying range

The market would expect a deal of this magnitude to net a rise of between 10 and 25%, based on the size of fffff, he could live with that he decided, lifting the phone to call his broker "John please" he said crisply to the girl who answered, "I'm sorry sir but John is not available at present".

"What do you mean not available at this time, John is my broker" he said with frustration in his voice, "One moment sir, who can I say is calling"?

"It is Henry, John knows me well". A male voice came on the line "Sorry about that Henry, this is Denis, one of the partners, John is in hospital I'm afraid". "In hospital, what is wrong with him, nothing serious I hope"?

"He was in a car crash two nights ago, he is bashed up somewhat, broken arms, legs and collar bone, he is awake and giving the poor old nurses a hard time, but no head injuries thank goodness".

"Can I help you with anything"? he asked. "I want to buy some shares".

"I can do that for you sir, what do you want to buy"?

"Buy 12 million shares at best of Fffff Company, and let me know when you have completed; do you want my phone number"?

"Of course not sir you are an old and very valuable client, I am so sorry about the telephonist, she is new". "It's ok Denis, phone me back".

The telephone rang softly, and was answered quickly "Denis here sir, I have purchased on your behalf 12 million shares in fffff, at an average price of 66 pounds, 15 pence", "Thank you" said the banker hanging up the phone

"One penny less than earlier, that will buy me a nice meal" he chuckled.

Now that the shares were safely in his name, he pondered whether to let Ralph in on the deal, he was a very big player, the shares he would buy, who knows how many millions, could drive the price even higher he pondered.

"Good morning to you Ralph, I have a deal for you if you are interested".

"Any deal from you must be good Henry, what have you got for me"?

Company fffff are making an offer to buy nnnnn any day now".

"I will not insult your integrity by asking you the obvious question, are you sure, I will just say thank you, and goodbye".

The news was announced in the afternoon, a bid was tabled, but a little haggling was going on behind the scenes, it was not yet accepted.

The markets closed with no further news of the take over.

The phone rang in the evening "Thank you for today Henry, I bought just in time, my spies tell me the deal will fly soon tomorrow, it looks like a good one, have you given any thought to the small jet plane".

"I have not had the time yet Ralph, but I will hire one of your Gulfstream for a couple of days, after you give me the B M date".

"You will find me not a bad friend to do business with Henry".

"As long as you win Ralph" he laughed "Of course" he replied, "is that not the reason why we don't sell cars for a living" he replied smoothly.

Another day dawned on the stock market, which was as frantic as ever, but the big news was the takeover by the giant construction company of another, if it succeeded, they would be the fourth largest in the world.

"Thank you Mildred I will skip breakfast this morning, just some toast and coffee will be fine".

Waiting was not one of his strong points; he doodled with his pen, drawing faces on a note pad, something he had not done since his University days, while he had waited for exam results.

Suddenly the news flashed across the TV screen, the takeover bid had been accepted, and the usual pandemonium that followed every large deal, occurred now as buyers and sellers fought to get the attention of the brokers.

The share prices rolled across the same screen in numerical order, the banker sat with bated breath, waiting for the stocks beginning with 'F'.

There it was, just over 91 pounds, the stock was flying, and he owned 12 million of them, he was ecstatic, and as rich as he ever dreamed or wanted to be, he had just made 300 million pounds.

"To hell with it, that is enough for me, I will let someone else make some money if it climbs any higher".

He picked up the phone "Denis, please sell at best, my 12 million shares in Fffff, and phone back when you have done so.

Feeling like celebrating, he thought, who with, his only true friend lived in London and he did not feel like driving all that way.

His wife and he were no longer married; she was probably married to someone else anyway by now.

He had an inspiration, "are you two interested in joining me for dinner at the best restaurant within 30 miles, or are the 'soapies' on TV too good".

"Excellent Jim, I will give you two hours to both get ready, we will take the Rolls, what do you say old chap, and by the way, I am putting fifteen million pounds into your account, the shares I bought for you paid off handsomely".

"How can we thank you Henry, you just keep giving us more and more money, and I do so little for you.

"Don't give it another thought James my boy, I am very happy with what you do for me, enjoy your wealth while you can".

During the sumptuous meal, the best in the County, the banker received a text message from Ralph "Hope you are celebrating as I am. I owe you one".

CHAPTER SEVEN

"HOW DO YOU TWO FANCY a couple of days in New York, you can bring a friend or your mother if you wish Colleen, as long as she has a current passport, you are going on a two day shopping spree, Jim and I have a job to do and then we will join you".

The three of them were sat in a restaurant; both had insisted on taking the banker out for a change.

"What airport are we flying from Henry, Heathrow"? Colleen asked.

"Actually my dear, we are flying from a small, airport in a private jet belonging to a friend of mine, a Gulfstream I believe it is called. I am also quite excited; it will be a first for me also".

"Can I bring my sister and my mother Henry".

"Of course my dear, as long as they have passports, but I have to ask, are they aware of Jim's condition, to put it delicately"

"We decided not to tell anyone, not even the kids. I visit them on my own and tell them all that that Jim is working away all the time, and that is where all the money comes from that they receive.

We just hope that one day Jim will wake up and be normal again, don't we" she said squeezing his hand

"So will you want to travel like you are now or invisible"?

"Like I am now of course, I feel great since you got me the new masks and contact lenses". "That reminds me Jim, I have ordered flesh coloured soft rubber gloves which are even fitted with finger and thumb nails so your hands will look normal, they go up to your elbows so you can buy him a new wrist watch Colleen". "Let me know if you like them Jim".

"The board meeting was scheduled for 2 pm next Tuesday, on the 77th floor of a skyscraper office block in Manhatton, New York.

"That really does sound like the big league to me" said Henry.

"Check the tape recorders and make sure we have new batteries Jim".

"Already done so chief, all ready to go" he replied.

The white Rolls pulled into the drive of the small house;

Henry was introduced to Colleen's mother and sister, whose eyes were wide open in astonishment, gaping at the white Rolls reverently.

Jim rode in the passenger seat, the three ladies sat in the rear "Are you all comfortable" asked the banker. "Are you joking, I am asleep already".

They arrived at the airport, which was larger than Henry had visualized, at least 100 small planes were parked, some were inside their hangers, and others parked on the concrete aprons, a few taxied to their positions, ready for take off. There were many different makes and sizes of aircraft; it was a vibrant and thriving industry.

Maneuvering the car into the parking bay indicated by the attendant, they collected their luggage and proceeded into the building, to be met by the clerk who was employed by Ralph to organize everything.

He shook hands, and took them through the formalities of customs and passport control, before escorting them to the sleek looking plane which stood on the tarmac. Climbing the portable steps, they settled into the soft leather seats, and looking around them, were impressed with the décor and the layout.

The pilot introduced himself "Hello my name is Greg, and this is my co pilot, Rex, we will be flying you to New York and back, if you need anything please ask, enjoy the flight".

The plane thundered down the runway and was quickly off the ground,

"So smooth, much better than the others I have flown to Spain in" said Jim, wearing his full regalia, including the new flesh coloured hands, which looked perfect. The banker noticed he had changed the old felt trilby, and now sported a white panama hat which looked good on him.

The three women were chattering non stop; Jim sat relaxed, his eyes closed. Henry, forever impatient to be active slid into a console housing a computer with Internet access, and became oblivious to everything around him, as his mind disappeared into the world of Finance.

"Lunch is ready ladies and gentlemen" said Rex, serving the gourmet food supplied by a caterer; the food was delicious, and served with any drink the passenger wished to name.

"This is the only way to travel" said Henry to himself, "I want one of these".

The small plane circled only once around the airport before coming to land smoothly, taxiing to its allotted parking place.

The small airport was situated 20 miles outside of the huge city of New York, but the close proximity to a five lane highway, guaranteed a swift journey to the city.

A courtesy car, sent by the hotel awaited their arrival; the burly driver approached "Welcome to the 'Big Apple', my name is Jed; I will take you to your hotel. He loaded their luggage into the trunk of the huge sedan, and joined the busy highway "What do you think of our city" he asked.

Looking up at the huge skyscrapers, it was difficult to not be impressed, and they told him so.

Arriving at the elegant five star rated hotel, they were greeted by a doorman, splendidly dressed in a maroon coloured morning suit, complete with top hat. "Good morning Y' all, welcome to our wonderful city, I hope you enjoy your stay".

Henry had booked a suite for two nights; the accommodation comprised three double bedrooms, each with an on suite bathroom, and a sitting room with its own TV

A large communal lounge with comfortable furniture and a huge bar completed the five star accommodations.

The best description would be opulent thought Jim looking around at the thick carpet, the beautiful paintings adorning the walls, and the crystal chandelier which hung in the centre of the room, with matching wall lights.

"Oh I could get used to this cooed Colleen's mum".

Seizing the opportunity to visit the world renowned places of interest, they took an open top bus tour of this very exciting city, and also sampled coffee and donuts in a street café, while watching the thousands of people scurrying past, heading to where only they knew.

Later they took a horse drawn cab which meandered slowly through Central Park, an unforgettable experience.

In the evening, Jim insisted on taking them out to dinner.

The five of them piled into one of the famous yellow taxi cabs "please take us to a restaurant that serves real Italian food" said Jim.

"Yes sir I know just the place, it is run by an Italian family, they are my cousins" he laughed. He was correct, the pasta, spaghetti, minestrone soup, bolognaise sauce, the meat balls, the red wine and the Italian ice cream, were all made by Italian hands, the meal was superb.

The next morning, after a wonderful breakfast, the three ladies went off in a taxi to enjoy their eagerly awaited shopping spree.

Armed with purses bulging with dollar bills, and credit cards as back up, they were in high spirits as the taxi pulled away, waving to the two men.

"We will walk and see if we can find the building where the meeting will be held, the map says two blocks".

Gazing up at the building which was so high it seemed to disappear into the clouds, Jim muttered "I have to go to the 77th floor, I may get a nosebleed".

They returned to the hotel where Jim changed into his invisible guise, strolling back, they reached the high building one hour early.

"Stay here Jim I will reconnoiter", he returned shortly, "All good, there are ten elevators which all go to the 92nd floor which is the top one, I will travel with you".

A security guard sat at a small desk, outside the meeting room, with a sheet containing the list of delegates, the door was closed, and Jim waited.

The first delegate arrived "Why is the door closed, we have a meeting here in half an hour" he said haughtily.

"The venue has been changed sir, the Japanese delegation is now much larger than we were told, a bigger room is required, and the board meeting has been moved to floor 86.

The delegate was not very pleased, and stormed off without a word to the guard "miserable sod" Jim heard the guard say, following the delegate to the elevator. "No Bob, don't bother getting out, press the button for the 86th floor, they have changed the meeting, thanks to the bloody Japs".

"Be careful with your mouth Paul, someone may hear you, they are not Japs, they are our partners, remember that", "I suppose so" mumbled Paul.

The invisible man stepped into the elevator with the two men.

The meeting room was huge, but even that was not large enough to seat everyone at the table; additional chairs had been put against the wall.

When the chairman entered, he had to squeeze past people to get to his seat. Jim found a spot behind the chairman and switched on the recorder, the Japanese delegates were so numerous, some even stood against the wall, a little too close to the invisible uninvited delegate for his liking.

This was the longest meeting that Jim had endured, some of the delegates spoke only Japanese, and an interpreter had to repeat everything in English.

"Good job I have two tape recorders, thanks to the banker" thought Jim.

The meeting lasted a full six hours; Jim was exhausted, standing in the same spot for all that time, listening to people arguing in English and Japanese took its toll, he had a splitting headache and he almost shouted out his joy when the chairman uttered the words "I declare this meeting closed".

"Gosh that was a long meeting" said the banker greeting him anxiously. "Henry just take the tapes please and don't speak to me, my feet ache and I have a splitting headache".

Jim and his wife Colleen invited everyone to dinner that evening, and beef steak was the preferred choice. Entering the taxi cab, Jim said "Cabbie will you please take us for the best steaks in New York".

"I know a good joint mister, the best T bones in the city, and the ribs aint bad either". He said. "My cousin will look after you, tell him Phil sent you".

So their visit to the 'Big Apple' ended with giant steaks, succulent ribs, onion rings and French fries, so tender, the meat fell off the bone.

The following morning, their luggage was taken away by the hotel staff, and the car waited to transport them to the airport.

They all left, vowing to return as soon as possible to the 'Big Apple'.

The white Rolls drove very slowly over the loose stones, and stopped outside the huge mansion.

Ralph himself walked out to greet the car "Hello Henry, good journey"?

"He produced the two tapes and handed them over. "Two tapes" he queried

"The meeting took six hours, half of it is in Japanese", the big man's jaw dropped, "Don't worry Ralph; an interpreter was also invited to the meeting". "I owe you big time Henry, you did great".

"Ralph that is my last deal, I have made all the money that I need, and I want to do different things with my life, I am now retired".

"What about whoever produced these" he said, holding up the tapes, "is that person available for hire". "Sorry, no Ralph, he and I are going to look at different things, but together".

"Mind if I ask what you are going into".

"All I will say is that it involves travel, maybe all over the world, but if I find anybody who needs finance, I promise I will call you".

Through the habit of many years, Henry checked the New York stock market; it was quiet at present. Later in the day he received a text message,

"Action about to start" it was sign R.

No further firm news, but rumours began to circulate about a huge deal in the city, which may involve Japan. The following day the financial markets in America and Japan exploded, as the news of a giant merger broke.

He switched off the computer and phoned Jim "Do you fancy a beer"?

"I am getting out of the finance business now, I want to look at something else, are you still hell bent on changing the world Jim"?

"I cannot abide savages who peddle drugs to kids, those who traffic them for prostitution and despot leaders who live like Pharos, while their people die from starvation. I once said to someone, why does god allow evil people to live, and do you know what he said". "I cannot imagine" said the banker.

"He said to me, god can not fight all the evil in the world that we have created all by himself, he needs a little help from us sometimes" he paused and took a sip of his beer. "Do you know Henry I cannot help but think god made me invisible so that I can help him to get rid of some of the rubbish in the world". Henry was silent, deep in thought; he sipped his wine before answering. "Those are fine words and I like your sentiments Jim, maybe you and I should make a list of the ones we might target, but I will not agree with anything too dangerous, I do not want to lose a good friend".

The next day Henry sat in the garden drinking coffee a helicopter hovered overhead, somebody waved to him from the cockpit but he could not make out who it was.

The 'copter landed nearby, and the burly figure of Ralph strode towards him.

"Good morning you retired banker, how are you this fine day, I thought I would pay you a surprise visit, I would like one of those please" he said pointing to the coffee. Henry waved to Mildred who was hanging out of the window "Mildred another coffee please".

"You are in a hell of a good mood old boy" he said

"I made a packet yesterday thanks entirely to you, and I just had to do something for you in return".

He continued "It was a difficult deal which needed all my concentration for two solid days; I could not let this chance of a lifetime pass me by, and I admit I forgot that you wanted a small piece of the action so I invested some on your behalf, this is your profit" he handed him a bankers draft for a little over 100 million dollars.

"Thank you Ralph that was kind of you" said Henry.

"One final thing, as a gift from me to you, I give you this" he said, handing over a large buff coloured envelope.

It was the ownership papers for the same Gulfstream aircraft that they had flown to New York in.

"Ralph I am utterly speechless, thank you so much" he stammered.

CHAPTER EIGHT

T HE TWO FRIENDS SAT TOGETHER discussing their next adventure.

"I think Southern Africa should be the first place we look at to be avenging angels" said Jim "I suggest we base ourselves in Johannesburg and have a look around, there is a despot around that area whom I do not like".

Explaining to his wife that he and Henry had three more projects to complete together, she asked no details, contenting herself with shopping trips to Milan and Paris with her sister and her mother "Just let me know when you have finished what it is you want to do" she said.

Henry had contacted Greg who agreed to join him full time with a 20% salary increase, Henry now owned his very own private jet so he could go wherever he wanted, he phoned Greg, we fly to Johannesburg tomorrow".

Landing in a small airport on the northern side of the city, they rented a car and booked into a four star hotel for one week until they had decided their next move. "I suggest we make contact with some news reporter from the local newspaper, they are usually good sources of knowledge.

Discovering where they 'hung out' was easy, and taking a table outside in the warm sunshine, they ordered two beers and after asking around casually, they were introduced to a senior reporter of the largest newspaper in the city.

They plied him with endless beers bought him a steak lunch, and he became a wonderful source of information.

Discussing the politics of Africa which was just up his street, he gave them his expert advice and opinions, which after hearing; they felt more confident that they understood the situation better.

"One for the road John", "not for me sport, I have to drive home" he said staggering to the toilet.

"Ok we know more than we did, I suggest we visit the country and see what things are like up there" said Henry.

Taking the scheduled flight from Johannesburg, they arrived at the airport and were surprised to see how large and modern it was.

Taking a taxi they traveled on tarmac roads, arriving at a modern looking hotel situated in the centre of the city.

The main streets were wide with well trimmed grass verges and gardens packed with flowers of different colours.

Rows of jacaranda trees sporting their blue flowers made a spectacular sight, contrasting with the beautiful red flowers of the Pride of India.

"Very impressive for any country, the gardeners here know what they are doing" said Jim in genuine admiration.

Walking into the impressive dining room the brilliant white table cloths hard to ignore, they noticed only three other guests.

"Every bloody thing is rationed" said a white guest, who had consumed three beers too many, "in the old days when whites ruled, the country, everything worked". His companion tried to keep him quiet, "shut up Hans you will cause trouble" he begged his friend.

"That bloody president cares nothing for his people" he shouted, and with that, his friend walked out of the hotel, got in his car and left.

"You seem upset" said Jim, moving next to him "so would you be if you had been born here and had to live in this place". "Then why don't you leave" said Jim. "And go where"? He said falling off the chair in a drunken stupour.

The meal was average, the meat was so tough, both questioned its origin, and left it uneaten, "never mind, the beer is nice and cold" said Henry.

"I think we need to hire a car and drive around the country to find out what the local people think" he continued.

"There is enough data on the Internet about this President, he has wrecked this country, given all the choice bits to his buddies, stolen all the money, and bought houses in Paris, he needs to go" said Jim.

"It is not the opinion of America or Britain, or readers of the Internet that matter, only what the locals think" said the ex banker.

They hired a car and drove around the country, seeing with their own eyes the devastation that had occurred.

The grass was all gone the roots had been chewed by the thousands of goats roaming the land, and the once renowned lush pastures were turning to dust.

"I read that the cattle that once roamed these fields produced the best beef in the world, and look at it now" he said shaking his head sadly.

Driving along the dusty roads made of sand with deep ruts everywhere; they saw the huts and small houses of an African village and decided to stop.

Approaching the largest dwelling, an old African came out to greet them.

"Sawubona, good day to you master" the old man said. "Good day to you, are you the leader"? "I am the tribal chief" he said, drawing himself up to his full height, showing the pride he still possessed, in spite of what the visitors may think of his present circumstances

"We are from overseas and are interested in learning how you live and if you are you happy" said Jim. The old man's eyes clouded over and he pulled the blanket he wore around his shoulders a little tighter "I have nothing to say to you, many people like you come from over the sea, they write books about how we live in poverty, make money for themselves, but our lives never change, go away and don't bother us" said the old warrior.

Following him to the door of the hut, Henry said "we mean you no harm and we are not here to cause trouble, we have come to help you if we can", pulling a handful of US $ notes out of his pocket, he thrust them into his hands. The old man looked around furtively "come inside before someone sees you" he hissed. He offered them a clay pot containing some liquid, both hesitated before bringing it to their lips, they found it quite pleasant, African beer made from millet.

The old chief took them to visit every member of the village; and they were appalled at what they saw.

Small children lay on straw mattresses, thin and weak, their arms and legs stuck out like matchsticks, eyes sunken into their heads, a look of hopelessness in them.

Many adults, also too sick and weak to stand up, lying there dying from malnutrition, the signs of sickness and misery could be seen everywhere in the village, it tore at the heart strings of the onlookers.

"You can see for yourself, need I say more", said the old chief.

"The money is a god send, it will buy the food and medicine that we need, god bless you, at least it shows that someone cares" he said, tears running down his ancient face.

"Answer me one question chief" said Jim, "What is your opinion of the president". "If I was given the chance, I would bury my spear deep into his chest" hissed the old warrior, with true anger in his eyes.

The two travelers suffered many emotions from the sights they had witnessed, a mixture of shock, sadness, horror, followed by anger.

"I need a large scotch" said the ex banker, "I will join you" Jim said.

Pulling over at the first hotel they saw, there were only a few customers.

"I have seen enough said Jim, I need to see how the President lives".

They had seen films of what the country had been like before this power mad President had grabbed the reins of the country, kept in power only by the mindless thugs who protected him.

"The people all had jobs and were happy before, why doesn't somebody do something about it, and get rid of this animal" cried Jim in anger.

"Because everybody is waiting for the white man to kill him" said a black man sat quietly in the corner, listening to every word.

"Why a white man" they asked him. "Because the truth is this country was much better when they were in charge, this butcher and thief cares nothing for the people, the whites would have taken him out years ago, but overseas opinion prevented them, and the truth is now, nobody cares".

"Will you join us please, I am Henry and my friend is Jim".

"My name is Ishmael" said the man, shaking hands.

"Things are not very good here then" said Jim.

"Keep your voice down, there are spies everywhere, it could mean big trouble for you" said Ishmael, placing his finger to his lips.

"The weather here is marvelous, much better than where we come from is that true Bill" said Jim to Henry with a wink, "Another round of drinks I think, does everyone agree"? He added jovially.

Finishing the drinks, they left a tip for the waiter, and motioned to Ishmael to follow them outside.

"Will you show us where the president lives Ishmael"?

"He has built himself a new Palace, I will not take you there, it is too dangerous for me, but I will show you the road that leads to it.

Follow me, I will put out my arm when I am ready to turn left, you will drive straight on, but you must be careful where you stop near his Palace his bullies will arrest you simply because of your white skin".

The African man smiled showing his white teeth "go with god" he said, offering his hand.

Ishmael drove a forty year old Austin 10, it spluttered and banged when he started the engine and clouds of black smoke rose in a column.

The two white men followed a long distance behind, in order to avoid the poisonous fumes belching from the exhaust.

Waving goodbye as he took a left turn, the road suddenly changed to tarmac and they knew that they were on the correct one.

Rounding a corner they were confronted by a road block.

Two large African soldiers dressed in khaki battle dress, each carrying AK47 assault rifles waved them to stop.

"This is a private road" said one. "Sorry we did not see a sign" said Jim.

"I repeat this is a private road" he said waving the rifle menacingly.

Henry quickly realized what he was after "Oh you mean it is a toll road" he said producing two ten $ bills.

This seemed to satisfy them, and they became friendlier, and even more so, when the white man offered them a cigarette, indicating to them that they could keep the pack.

"We are on holiday in your beautiful country, is there any chance of taking some photographs of the Presidents Palace"? Asked Jim.

"Hello what is in his mind"? Thought Henry, who had noticed a change in the attitude of his invisible friend of late, he was much more confident.

"No you are not allowed, but maybe we could turn a blind eye if another one of these was offered" said the more senior of the two with a sly look.

"Show us the Palace first" said Jim firmly.

The soldiers hopped into their army jeep and drove down the road, then appearing from nowhere was the sight of a huge Palace.

A huge white painted structure consisting of five different roofs, each with a spire, and covered in black tiles, and pink painted windows, it stood gleaming against the backdrop of a deep blue sky and bright sunshine.

It looked like something out of a Walt Disney film, but ridiculously out of place against the stark landscape of Africa

Jim gazed at this opulent monstrosity and felt physically sick, thinking what it must have cost the tax payers of the country.

"How wonderful "he pretended, "can we park here"?

"For $20 each, we will give you 30 minutes" said the guard.

"Where will you be" said Jim, "At the post where we were" he said.

"Agreed" said Jim producing two $20 bills.

"What are you up to Jimbo", "Never mind Henry I will tell you later" he said peeling of his mask and clothes, and becoming invisible.

Passing by the many guards, most of them lolling carelessly against the walls, he walked through the front door of this fairy grotto, and surveyed the pantomime scene before him.

More than 200 people sat in a vast dining room, the tables covered with expensive table cloths were laden with food, so heavy that the legs groaned under the weight, threatening to collapse.

Whole sheep, pigs and goats had been roasted over coals by the many chefs, who were now busy carving the carcasses for the enjoyment of the guests.

Huge racks of beef, pork sausages, livers, tripe, hearts, kidneys and heads, all delicacies loved by African people, sat on silver trays which were delivered to the tables by dozens of sweating, overworked waiters.

Hundreds of chickens had been cooked by the chefs, browned to perfection. The friends, family and business associates of the President, fortunate enough to be invited to this feast, chatted happily and laughed loudly, dressed in their expensive clothes and wearing priceless jewelry, they devoured the food with gusto, the leftovers were aimlessly thrown to the dogs belonging to the president.

The invisible man made his way to the head of the table, where sat the President of this banana republic, all 240 kilos of fat and blubber.

The large shaven head held the smallest, beadiest eyes that Jim have ever seen, thick lips surrounded the huge mouth, which devoured food in prodigious quantities, chomping it like a hippopotamus.

Jim felt ill just watching this exhibition of gluttony and wanton greed, he thought about the small children not too many miles away, lying in cots and dying of starvation, his blood boiled with anger.

"How could god allow such people to live and get away with murder" he remembered it being said, and also the reply, "god cannot rid the world of all the rubbish that we have created, he needs some help from mankind" he whispered to himself.

On the huge plate in front of the despot sat three whole roasted chickens, the invisible assassin took one, tore off a leg, reaching round the head of the fat man with his left arm he pinched the nostrils of his nose as tightly as he could, and as he opened his mouth to suck in air, the assassin pushed the whole chicken leg into his mouth with his right hand, forcing it deep down into his throat, then hitting it with the heel of his hand to make sure that it was jammed solid.

The evil president started to choke, his face turning purple, nobody noticed his plight as they were all too busy gorging themselves, and the gurgling sounds he made were not heard until it was too late, and he was dead.

Pandemonium broke out; someone tried to revive the president who had fallen with his face into his plate of food.

Jim heard behind him, the wailing of African women and the ululations which only they can make, as he walked quickly away from the palace.

Dressing quickly, he told his friend quietly "Get out of here Henry, the president is dead, but he died of natural causes".

Fearing that the government would close the airport when the news got out, he phoned Greg "Bit of trouble here, can you come and get us please".

Deciding to spend some time in South Africa after traveling all this way, Henry flew to the game reserve accompanied by Greg; Jim decided that he wanted to relax around the swimming pool of the hotel.

Using the satellite phone he called Ralph "where are you said the wealthy financier". "Sat having a glass of wine in Kruger Park with an

Elephant sat on my knee". "I heard there were some large women out there, but not that big" he chuckled. "What's the news Henry"?

"You may have heard about the death of the President just up the road from here, the newspapers are full of it here, saying there could be big changes coming, I have a feeling that a good Investment banker may be needed very soon, would you be interested"?

"I am always interested; like the Windmill Theatre in the war old boy, I never close, how long are you staying "? "Two weeks, at least".

"I think I might join you for a few days".

"This is the life Greg. Don't you think" said Henry watching the monkeys in the trees and the Impala crop the grass 100 meters away, drinking a glass of chilled champagne.

"Very much sir, thank you for inviting me".

"Not sir, Greg, Henry will do nicely, I am not all that old you know".

"It has nothing to do with age Henry, just respect for you".

Based on what the South African newspapers were saying, Henry had not forgotten John the black reporter whose articles he read every day, he really hit the nails right on the head with some of them, they were good.

He recalled the proud old African warrior to whom he gave $, and Ishmael with his old Austin 10, he smiled at the memory and wondered how they were feeling after the death of the hated president.

According to John's articles a new government was about to be formed, headed by the leader of the opposing party, a man popular with all.

"The many millions stolen by the dead President would be brought back and invested where it belonged.

Many of the president's henchmen had been arrested, and forced to bring back their stolen millions.

A man such as Ralph would be perfect to advise on the investments, and to finance the new industries which were needed to bring the country off of its knees and back to its former glory.

All this was put into an email and sent to Ralph, he would know what to do.

His friend, Jim, the invisible assassin had certainly done the world a big favour, in this small part of it at least.

Sat in the cockpit of his own plane for the first time, he thrilled at the spectacular view, also enjoyed by the pilot who sat in the next seat.

What a wonderful view Greg, thank you for inviting me".

My pleasure Henry, and I really mean that sir" he laughed.

Arriving back at the hotel he found Jim was now totally relaxed; he seemed to be a different person, particularly since his escapade up north.

"How are you Jim" asked his friend. "Fine Henry" he replied.

"I mean how are you on the inside, after the great service you did".

"I am fine Henry; really, I feel that god is happy that I helped him a little".

"So do I, Jim, I am also proud of you and what you did".

CHAPTER NINE

ACK IN HIS FAMILIAR AND much loved study, Henry found himself being drawn more and more to the study of the bad side of life, the world of crime.

It covered a wide range, from the manufacture, distribution and sale of narcotics, the awful trade in trafficking young children into prostitution and even slavery, to corruption, the stealing of money from banks and institutions, which affected the savings of working people.

All are evil crimes; and it is not possible to say which the worst is.

"It would be wonderful if it were possible to send out a policeman, arrest every one of the bad guys and lock them up, then everything will be good" thought Henry, "Dream on" he added.

"Does god really need some help from mankind to get rid of the bad people?

Possibly, but what about the most evil of all crimes, greed.

How do you get rid of that crime, maybe use an invisible assassin"?

Deciding that the subject was too wide and too complicated to be considered alone, he felt that he needed the opinions of his friend.

"I have started making lists, but I need your input for our next projects Jim, would you like to join me for lunch, or just join me".

"Of the three hated crimes I think we should concentrate on one Jim, maybe the narcotic trade is where we should start, what do you think"?

"Yes it is as good as any I must admit Henry, I do not know where to start, not even which country to consider.

Drug dealers don't exactly advertise in the yellow pages do they"?

"The thing about drug dealing which makes me really angry is giving it to children in order to get them hooked, that is the lowest of the low for me".

"Maybe we start there Henry I agree with you. I have the advantage of being invisible, so I can be more effective".

"I have decided how I may be able to make a small difference, but it can only be me who can do it, because I cannot be seen".

"What do you have in mind, pray tell" said his good friend.

"I am going to do what you are not able to do, watch a school, and catch a dealer handing out free drugs to young kids in order to get them hooked on the filth that they peddle, maybe I will be lucky and catch one".

"That sounds a good idea, but please be careful, the animals who deal in drugs are usually violent people, don't get caught".

Jim drove his own car to the area that he had selected; he went into a public house and ordered a pint of beer.

Casually walking into the toilet, he took off his clothes, and hid them well.

Taking a tour around the perimeter of the school several times, he saw nothing untoward, nor any suspicious characters.

The cars of parents collecting their children began to arrive, "time to call it a day" he decided. The work he had taken on was frustrating, asking the parents would be of no help, they would know nothing, and he could hardly ask the children, or could he, suddenly having an idea.

The following day he walked into the playground as the children came outside for their break.

He mingled with the children, making sure to keep a safe distance, but near enough to overhear the chat between them.

His ears pricked up at a word he heard clearly, the word "dealer" from one boy to another, sidling close he listened to their conversation.

"I tell you the dealer said he will be around the school tomorrow, he will sell you some speed if you want some and you might even get a free sample".

Looking at the boys very closely so he would remember their faces, he decided that tomorrow would be the day.

Circling slowly around the school playground, he guessed that any contact with the pupils would be during their break.

He saw an expensive looking vehicle parked on the other side of the school, he headed there and watched.

A man, with his hair plastered close to his scalp, wearing an expensive looking suede jacket, walked casually to the perimeter fence and lit a cigarette; he walked along the path next to the road and back again.

Hundreds of children appeared in the playground, some shouting in excitement as they started to kick a football.

Jim saw the same two boys that he saw yesterday, plus two more, casually walk to the small wall with the high chain link fence on top, where the man in the suede jacket stood, smoking another cigarette.

"Hi guys" he said, greeting the boys "are these two interested in trying out my product"? They nodded and he passed two small packets through the fence, "I will be back next Tuesday for your orders, but no more free samples, it will be cash on the nose, my prices are the lowest and the product is the best you will find anywhere".

Jim ran to the mans car, he had a dilemma, he could not run to his own car to follow him, he could hardly drive a car in his present state, deciding that he had no option, standing at the passenger door as the man arrived at his car.

Suddenly deciding his first idea was not a good one, he noted the license number and the make and colour of the vehicle, standing back as it drove off, accelerating quickly away.

Arriving at the same venue next Tuesday, there would be no mistakes.

The expensive car arrived, he got out, it was the same man, but this time he wore an Italian leather jacket he went to the fence and waited.

Jim had brought his camera and took several snaps of him and the car.

"Just in case they may be needed" he told himself.

The children came out as usual; the four boys joined the man at the fence.

He took several photographs of the boys, packets and money changing hands, the invisible man started his car and followed the drug dealer as he drove away, just managing to keep him in sight.

Making many stops, and meeting several people, the dealer was a busy man, all were recorded on camera.

Stopping at a takeaway, he took a packet of food into the car and drove off, this time he stopped outside a block of flats and locked the car.

Jim followed, made a careful note of the flat number, went behind a wall and became invisible, taking a baseball bat from the boot of his car, he made sure that nobody was in sight, and knocked on the door.

The drug dealer opened the door furtively, and seeing no one there, he stepped outside to have a better look, giving Jim his opportunity to step inside the apartment.

As he expected, it was furnished with very expensive things.

"A good business to be in, dealing drugs" he said aloud.

"What the, who is there" shouted the dealer in a panic stricken voice.

"Wouldn't you like to know you dealer in death" answered Jim.

This action almost cost him his life by being too arrogant and cocksure of himself, just because he was invisible did not make him immune to bullets, the drug dealer produced a pistol, entering the room he waved it menacingly, ready to fire at anything he saw.

Fortunately for the invisible man, the baseball bat was hidden from the drug dealer's sight, he lifted the bat and brought it crashing down on his skull, he collapsed, unconscious.

"That was a bad mistake "he told himself harshly," one I will never repeat".

He picked up the phone and dialed a number previously researched.

"May I speak to the drug squad please, yes this is flat number 322 Mews Green, there is a large party next door and they are all smoking drugs, the smell is awful come quickly please" he hung up.

He heard the sirens, the Police entered the flat when they saw that the door was wide open, and the drug dealer sat in a chair facing them, with a large sign around his neck "I am a dealer who sells filthy drugs to children, the evidence is in my pockets and hidden in this flat".

The officer said "I wonder who set this up for us".

"I have no idea" said another "but I would sure like to shake his hand".

Jim printed all the evidence he had filmed, including the four young boys, who would be punished, but hopefully would not end up as drug addicts.

A large envelope was left at Police reception, it contained all the photos.

"Now I call that a good days work and a small help for god" said Jim.

He repeated the same exercise on twelve more occasions, resulting in the arrest and conviction of twelve more peddlers of drugs to children, and twelve schools made safer for the pupils and their parents.

"How do you feel after doing all that good work Jim".

"Like an avenging Angel Henry, a wonderful feeling".

CHAPTER TEN

"THOSE WERE THE EASY DRUG dealers we put behind bars, what about going for just one of the big boys Henry, do you think it is possible".

"In my honest opinion it is time to make yourself known to the head lads of the Drug Squad, they will welcome you with open arms after the work you just saved them, and the credit they have received".

"Yes I think you are probably right, I will make contact with them and see what they have to say, do you want me to include you Henry"?

"If I can be of use to you Jim, without making me invisible, yes" he laughed.

"Oh and don't forget, we are a registered detective agency, we can use that".

Henry picked up the phone "May I speak to the chief of the Drug Squad please", "my name does not matter, but my friend gave you the thirteen drug peddlers who targeted schools, yes, that's the one".

"Good afternoon officer may I know who I am speaking to please"?

"Chief Inspector Nolan, wonderful sir, my friend and I would like a meeting with you, we would like to assist you with your job, if you will allow us".

"Yes I understand that, we just want to chat, would you mind a nice restaurant, and I am paying. Good, thank you."

"Jim we are meeting a C I Nolan of the Drug Squad for lunch tomorrow, you happy about that"?

"So Chief Inspector", "Please call me Trevor" he replied. "Great, I am Henry and he is Jim, what would you like to drink"?

"Trevor you are not on duty, this is a business meeting".

"You could call us Philanthropists I suppose, but we are a bit better than that, we are rich enough to not have to work anymore and we both detest crime, like selling narcotics, people trafficking and despots who ruin their own countries", "Yes we read about that one in Africa, we enjoyed that one very much, he died of natural causes, a chicken bone got stuck in his throat I believe" said the C I.

"Yes we read that also, anyway Trevor, we would like to help if we can".

"Henry the big boys are utterly ruthless and will stop at nothing to peddle their filth, and there are no shortages of customers at any price they want to charge, there are so many addicts in the world now, I can take you to places that will make you weep.

We know who the big fish are, but they are protected by big politicians, who receive millions in bribes most likely.

"What if we are prepared to risk our necks to get you the evidence to help you convict, would that help"? said Jim, speaking quietly.

Trevor stared at him intently; there was something about this man that made you believe what he said. "Jim it will be dangerous to even talk about these savages, let alone go after them" it was evident that he loathed them.

"I had a young sister who died of a heroin overdose" he lied.

"Tell me, how did you apprehend those thirteen drug peddlers at the schools that was brilliant work"? said the policeman.

"Persistence and a little bit of good luck, it wasn't all that wonderful" he said

"We are grateful to you, and that reminds me, I still want to shake your hand" he said, offering his hand, which Jim shook.

Henry brought himself back into the discussion "Trevor, neither Jim nor I are willing to take on anything more dangerous than what your squad handle, quite frankly we are not in your league, it's just that we have many contacts from the successful businesses which Jim and I ran, we do have our own detective agency and have some good men work for us" he lied.

"I still don't understand what you are both looking for from me".

"Tell us the names of a couple of the big boys, and where to find them, if we can help with our resources we will say so, if not, we forget the whole idea".

"Don't misunderstand us Trevor, we both hate crime with a passion, and we will do anything we can to assist you, and we do have many contacts".

"So do I hate crime and I am impressed with your honesty, come to my office next week, I will introduce you to some of my team and we will see if there is anything that you can do to help us catch just one of these animals.

"May I have more wine please; I have never drunk any as good as this".

Later as they both sat in Henry's sun lounge Jim said to his friend

"Thank you for what you did today, you are a very clever man Henry, you have understood my need to bring down a few of the world's bad men, we can only get a fraction of them I know, but even that may make a difference"

The phone rang "You will be pleased to know I arrived back from Africa yesterday, and I have made some wonderful contacts, believe it or not, they offered me the position of Minister of Finance in the new Government, I declined of course but I have agreed to be a part time advisor".

"Good to hear your voice again Ralph, I am glad it worked out well for you in Africa, I found them to be delightful people, I hope the new President does a better job than the last one" said Henry.

"I just phoned to thank you again for thinking of me, what are you up to Henry"? "Not much really, just dabbling a bit here and there, it would not interest you Ralph".

"How is your new plane, any plans for further trips"?

"I absolutely love it, I am toying with another trip back to the States soon, I would like to visit Miami, and definitely spend a few days in New York".

The two would be detectives were introduced to some hardened professional detectives by their well respected boss.

"Gentlemen I would like you to meet the two people who gave our department the thirteen dealers, all wrapped up in neat parcels" said the drug squad Chief "say hello to Jim and Henry".

"Gentlemen, these are my two best men Alan and Frank".

Frank who was the senior of the two spoke "Trevor has filled us in on what you gents are looking for, and we sure appreciate your help, I want to start by taking you on a tour so you realize what you are up against, how bad the drug problem really is, and how evil these people are".

A Drug Rehabilitation Centre was the first place visited, and the two amateurs were shown young people as young as ten who were addicted to hard drugs, forced upon them by ruthless, greedy, so called human beings.

Speaking to the doctors, even they admitted it was a difficult job to wean them off the powerful drugs, which in some cases they would fail.

"What drugs do to a family is terrible" the doctor told them "It can be the father, the mother, or the children who are addicted, I have seen cases where the whole family are addicted, and have no choice but to sell the stuff to others in order to survive. Eventually they end up taking an overdose or some bad stuff that kills them". He said sadly. "It is a rotten shame".

The Detectives then took the two to a local hospital that specialized in injuries caused by violence, whether it be gunshots, knives or badly beaten the injuries in this hospital were very severe.

Frank explained "the people who end up in here are usually people who owe money to the dealers and cannot pay, dealers starting up their business in somebody else's area, you get the picture, but they are animals, and make their own rules" he said, "Our job is to catch them and put them away for a long time" he added. "We welcome any help you can give us".

They took the detectives for a nice lunch, accepting that they only drank fruit juice.

"You could help us by doing some surveillance work, we simply do not have the manpower, we will give you a list of what we want, but you must report back to us, we are not deputizing you as sheriffs to hunt them down" he grinned at his joke. "Agreed" chorused the two.

"Without realizing it, they have given us exactly what we need, spying is what we do best" said Jim. "They will eventually lead us to the top men, and we are in a better position than them to decide how to deal with them".

The drug squad had given them one name to start, a well known psychopath called Jericho who was alleged to be the head of all the dealers who sold to customers; they admitted that they did not know how many dealers he controlled, Jericho worked for a Drug Lord whom they did not name.

The invisible man walked through the door of the large house by following one of the drug dealers, Jim saw him enter a room and he followed.

"Hi Jericho, here is the money from the last shipment I sold, and a list of what I need to supply my clients, I calculate you owe me thirty eight thousand, I will wait in the bar" he said, moving into the next room where two others sat, and a good looking woman sat behind the bar.

"Hi Rose, give me a beer please, hi boys" he greeted the other two.

Jim had his tape recorders and was taping everything that he heard, standing next to the group he left the tape running, to be heard and deciphered by others. Jim wandered back into the first room where the large man, who must be Jericho, sat. The man was a cruel looking individual with several scars on his face, and a nose that had been broken more than once.

He sat at a computer which Jim noted with interest contained a list of names and columns of figures, this was exactly what Jim was after, and he would find a way to extract the information from the computer, or he would steal the whole computer if necessary. Jim had not noticed before, but a man stood in a corner, hidden by a curtain, holding an Uzi sub machine pistol.

Surveying the room, he noticed there were two doors leading to other rooms, and trying them both, discovered both were locked.

The door of one room opened and a man shouted "Jericho here is the money for Slim, thirty eight thousand on the nose; it is correct what he paid in".

Eventually the second door was unlocked, "Jericho here is the fresh supply of 'snout' that Slim requested".

Jim followed the dealer called Slim as he walked to the reinforced steel door; and he was let out by the gangster who toted the Uzi.

"My god this is another world" said the invisible man, who had seen enough for one day, he had plenty to report back to Henry with, the names on the computer he would solve at a later date, but for now, he was hungry.

"As usual your work is first class" enthused Henry; you have done more in a day than others could do in months". "Don't forget I have a slight advantage over others Henry, how long will Mildred be with dinner, I am starving".

After dinner the two would be detectives relaxed in the lounge.

"This house I was in today is full of drug dealers; they just walk in and out as they please, and nobody stops them, I can see why the drug squad gave us this to watch, I could spend months going in every day and seeing the same thing, but that is not what I am looking for, I want the top boy who pulls all the strings, and makes all the money, and I think the Jericho character will lead me to him". "Jim please be careful, the drug squad have told you how dangerous they are'.

The next day, the invisible man decided to explore the whole house and see exactly what went on inside.

Climbing the stairs, he was confronted by security fencing made from 20 mm diameter steel bars, and a gate made from the same material.

There was no alternate way to access whatever lay behind the bars, even for the invisible man, he was about to admit defeat when the wooden door which lay beyond the gate was opened.

A man dressed in white clothes, even white boots and wearing a mask, took out a packet of cigarettes, lowered the mask and lit one.

He had left the door behind him wide open, and Jim had a partial view of what lay beyond.

"A huge laboratory for making their own drugs, right here on the premises, how ingenious is that"? He whispered in grudging admiration.

Having discovered all there was to see upstairs, he then explored the rest of the ground floor. Beyond the bar, he saw living accommodation "Seems like Jericho and the bar lady live together" he deduced.

A passage led to the back door, which he could see through the glass panels led to a secluded garden with high walls, and a large separate building, obviously a garage to house two cars.

He tried the door, it was locked, he saw some keys hung on a hook.

Trying one in the lock, the door opened without a sound, there were two identical looking keys so he tried the other, just to be sure, it worked.

Slipping one of the keys into an invisible pocket "One never knows when that could become useful".

He spied a door at the end of a smaller passage which he had not noticed, the door opened silently at his touch, and he could see nothing, only blackness.

Feeling the wall he discovered a light switch, and the single bulb illuminated the stone steps leading to a basement.

Closing the door behind him, he descended cautiously, extracting the small powerful torch which he always carried from a pocket.

Another light switch produced a sight which sent shivers down his spine.

A small table and a solitary chair were the only furniture, but hung from hooks all down one wall, were numerous weapons of torture.

He saw electric wires, with plugs to fit into the wall socket, a rack full of razor sharp knives, hammers, pliers, coils of steel wire, lengths of rope, clubs made of solid wood, and a leather whip.

To complete the sight, which made the invisible man's stomach churn, there was a small room with a single bed with mattress, behind steel bars.

"In the name of heaven, how can this be allowed to happen in a civilized country, what kind of people are these"?

Before he was able to examine any further, his heart missed a beat as a loud voice rang out from the top of the steps "who the hell left the light on, is anyone down there"?

Many thoughts flashed through Jim's mind, the man would turn out the light and lock the door, leaving him a prisoner here for how long he wondered, until the next victim was dragged into this torture chamber perhaps, he may starve to death before then.

Recovering his senses he told himself to keep calm, the man at the top of the steps had to come down to turn out this light.

Jericho descended the stone steps, a fearsome look on his face, his heavy shoes with steel toe caps making a loud noise on the bare concrete "it could only be me, stupid fool that I am, only me comes down here" he said.

Heaving a huge sigh of relief, the invisible man slipped passed him, his rubber soled shoes making no noise as he mounted the stairs two at a time.

The dangerous looking man inserted a key into the lock, then walked back to his place of work, Jim shivered again at what could have been.

CHAPTER ELEVEN

I T WAS NECESSARY FOR JIM to be patient, until what he waited for, happened.

Every day he waited outside until a dealer arrived, followed him inside, and hoped there would be a change in the routine.

This day he could feel something different would occur.

He heard Jericho singing loudly in the shower, he emerged wearing a smart brown suit, matching tie, smelling of after shave he kissed the woman

"I am off to the monthly meeting with the boss, don't wait up doll, I may be a little late" he said, adjusting his hat in the mirror.

Jim's excitement grew as he followed the big man down the passage and out of the back door, he bent down, lifted the garage door and walked to an immaculate brown Oldsmobile, polishing a spot of dust on the bonnet with his handkerchief before getting inside, he turned the key and the huge engine fired into life, quickly settling down into a quiet hum, increasing as the driver eased the huge vehicle out of the garage, and stopping to get out to close the garage door, gave Jim his chance, he opened the back door, slid onto the seat, carefully pulling the door closed so only a soft click was heard.

Jericho drove the beautiful car at a fast speed; the automatic gears could hardly be felt as the huge machine took every hill with ease.

They drove along a two lane road that Jim recognized, entered a roundabout, and the huge machine accelerated away at a tremendous speed, a shout from the driver told him that Jericho was enjoying driving his pride and joy.

"That's it my baby go" he cried as the speedometer recorded 140 mph.

The familiar wail of the police siren behind him, told him slow to down or he would be in even greater trouble, he pulled over.

"So sorry officer I just never realized how fast I was going".

"You were doing 142 mph to be exact sir, afraid that is a court appearance".

"Oh well what are lawyers for" he said, taking the ticket.

He drove more sedately now; drawing up at a large wrought iron gate, a security guard approached the driver's window to check who it was.

Recognizing the man, he pressed a button to open the huge gates and the car slid slowly down the drive, parking with the dozens of other cars.

Jim opened the back door at exactly the same moment as Jericho opened his, hoping that he would not notice, closing his at the same time, he waited.

The drug dealer shook hands with some others who had just arrived.

"Hello Lefty good to see you again, howzit going with you"?

"Not bad Jericho, but business is a little slow" he complained.

They entered the huge mansion together, depositing the hand guns that all of them carried through a small window, receiving a numbered ticket as a receipt, then submitting to a body search, before being allowed to enter the huge bar with the many others.

A gong sounded, and the visitors filed into a huge dining room to enjoy a sumptuous lunch.

The invisible uninvited guest even managed to have lunch, seeing an unattended full plate left for one minute while the waiter went back to the kitchen for a sweet, Jim quickly took the plate, with utensils, he ducked into an empty room to enjoy a succulent steak.

The waiter returned, scratching his head, where did he leave the plate he wondered, and then throwing his hands in the air as if to say what does it matter, he went back to the kitchen and took another.

Two hours later, lunch was over and a man rang a bell asking for quiet, announcing that the meeting with the big boss would start in ten minutes.

The delegates trouped into a large meeting room and took their seats.

Jim switched on his trusty tape recorder, he counted 36 delegates.

Expecting a huge person, he was surprised to see a small man, no more than five feet two inches, or 1meter, 57 cm, and weighing only 112 pounds, 51 kg walk to the centre of the stage.

He had long, dark hair, was dark skinned, and boasted at least six gold teeth

The accent, when he spoke, sounded to be from a South American country.

"Good evening my friends, welcome to our little get together, I hope you all had a pleasant journey to get here. First I will give you the good news, the sales of our products were at a record high last month, which means of course record earnings for us all".

Applause rang around the hall as he continued. "Now we have the bad news, it was necessary to terminate the positions of three of our members for stealing from me" silence had fallen on the gathering, the big boss went on "I will tell you honestly, they were hung upside down and their throats were cut, just like animals, that is the punishment for any who try to steal from me, Carlo.

Understand me all of you, I decide the prices you will sell at, and I decide what commission you earn, you do not decide this. We are a family, and when you agreed to join the family, it is for life and you cannot leave, I will not let you leave" he screamed, "you know too much".

Realizing that he may have gone too far, Carlo softened his voice which became laughing and friendly "My friends do you not become rich working for Carlo"? The hall broke into large cheers; the audience smiled, patted each other on the back and clapped their leader.

"My friends let me introduce you to my four assistants, all family like you" he said, and four swarthy young men waved to the crowd.

Jim, who stood only yards away, saw what these young men were, bodyguards yes, but also hired killers; he could see it by the lithe and smooth way they moved, and the bulges under their jackets told its own story.

This small figure on the stage was so powerful, he had the status of a Mafia Godfather and he controlled the flow of narcotics, not because he was smart, but because he was also utterly ruthless, this was a dangerous man.

The meeting ended, and the guests, who were mostly hoodlums themselves, piled into the bar, determined to have a good night. As the alcohol flowed, a fight broke out between two of the members, and the speed and force of only one of the bodyguards in putting them both down, was awesome.

The invisible man knew if he did not seize this opportunity to eradicate this drug lord tonight, there would never be another one.

He did not have a specific plan, he decided to wait, and see if one came.

The small build of the leader would cause no problem to him, thought Jim, he was nothing without his bodyguards, and if he could catch him on his own, without their protection, there was a chance to take him out.

He concentrated only on Carlo, and followed him wherever he went.

The leader of probably the largest drug empire in the world had no idea that he was being shadowed by an invisible enemy.

Jim saw that one of the young bodyguards never took his eyes off his boss, following him everywhere that he went.

Carlo headed for his private study, nobody was allowed in without an invitation, Jim followed closely, and if he closed the door behind him without allowing the guard in, this was his big chance. He closed the door.

Jim silently slid in place the bolt of the door, no one could now enter.

He had collected some drug samples from Jericho's house, intending to use them as evidence, but he had a much better use for them now.

Recalling the terrible sights he had been shown of young children shaking and vomiting while under the influence of these awful drugs, sold without a glimmer of conscience, just to swell an already vast fortune and to retain the power that he could not exist without, Jim's blood boiled, the gorge rose into his throat, and his anger became too strong to resist. He grabbed the small arms, and tied them together with plastic ties, then looped a chord around his neck, tying it securely to the back of his hi back chair.

"What the hell, who are you" stammered the drug baron, fear in his voice.

"I am an avenging Angel sent by God". "What do you mean, I can see no one" he cried. "Exactly my drug dealing friend, I have been sent on an errand to pay you back for all the people you have murdered, and he also made me invisible so I could do it better".

"I will give you all the wealth you have ever dreamed of if you let me go".

"Thanks but I have all the wealth that I need".

"I do not ask the people to buy my drugs; they buy them because they want to, they enjoy them". "Is that why your goons give them free to small children to get them hooked on the filthy stuff, and become your prisoner for the rest of their life, or take an overdose and die"?

"What are you going to do" he said in a whimpering voice.

"I am going to give you some free samples of your own product" he said, grabbing his nose, waiting until he opened his mouth to gasp for air, and pushing a handful of assorted pills into his mouth, and forcing him to swallow. Taking a glass of water the invisible assassin poured it into his mouth, most of it ended in his stomach.

The drugs started to take effect on the drug baron; he let out a crazy laugh, and babbled some nonsense.

"Time to leave now" said Jim, sliding back the bolt and opening the door.

The bodyguard jumped to attention, then seeing his boss in distress, he ran to his side, allowing the invisible man time to make his escape.

Henry collected the tapes, typed all the details as Jim dictated, and they produced a very comprehensive report to give to the drug squad.

The drug baron did not die, his aides managed to get him to hospital in time for them to pump out his stomach, however he remained very ill.

"I need to speak to Carlo" said Jim. "What, you mean the drug baron"?

Said Henry, "Whatever would you want to speak to him for"?

"Just an idea I have, I will be back soon".

"Hello Carlo, it's me again", the small swarthy man's eyes rolled with fear, and he tried desperately to reach the bell push to call for help.

Jim put his arm on his shoulder "I come in peace, I want to help you".

"I would have you killed if I could reach my guard" he hissed.

"Hear me out Carlo, I have an idea, if you do not like it, I will go away".

"Do I have a choice" he said, pointing to the drips connected to him.

"Look, your organization is finished, the police will soon raid your house and all of your dealer's houses, and you will spend the rest of your life in prison, is that what you want"?

"My lawyers will have me out in two hours" he said.

"Not this time my friend, the evidence is too strong, and some members of your 'family' will sing like canaries to save their own skin, you know it".

"What do you have in mind, I am listening".

"You have caused much harm to many people, and no doubt have amassed a lot of money, so why not use your money to make amends and start giving back to society. "How"? He asked. "By using your huge wealth to fight against drugs". "Will they allow me to walk away from the charges"?

"I have some very good contacts in the drug squad, I will speak to them".

"They will want you to divulge all your contacts, where the drugs come from, and how you move them around the world".

"I will then have many enemies, who will protect me"? He asked quietly.

"I will" said Jim "I will become the invisible avenger" he laughed, but he was serious. "You would do this for me, a drug baron"?

"Yes I would Carlo, because you would become my friend, we can work together with many good people, and do some good for the world, better living like this than looking over your shoulder for the rest of your life."

"When I was young in Bogota, it was easier to deal in drugs than not".

"Speak with your people invisible man; I do not even know your name"

"My name is Jim, I believe we will become friends Carlo, like another that I once tried to kill, he is now my best friend".

They held a meeting with members of the drug squad, who were ecstatic when they realized the sheer size of the deal which had just been given to them on a plate; they were particularly impressed with the evidence, the tape recordings, names, dates and sworn evidence.

"How the deuce did you manage all this in such a short time" said Trevor.

"We have some good people working for us, and we have access to the best surveillance equipment that maybe you don't have" said Henry modestly.

They readily agreed not to prosecute Carlo, in return for the huge amount of information he had already given them, and further agreed that his name would be kept confidential and not to appear in the press.

"One last thing said Trevor, a small matter of the 2.4 million pounds in reward money coming your way for the recovery of such a huge value of drugs" "Where does that money come from" asked Jim. "Private companies, sponsorships the government". "Are you able to collect this money"?

"Of course and then hand to you, in a press conference".

"You have a charity for the widows and orphans of police who lose their lives don't you"? He asked. "Yes", well give it to them with our blessing" he said looking at his friend who nodded his head in agreement.

CHAPTER TWELVE

"You know what, we all need a nice holiday, I own a private jet, and we made a few bob on the Stock Market, so where do you all want to go"?

"What about back to New York, we all enjoyed it last time".

"Ok, New York it is" said Henry, "how many will be going".

"Colleen, myself and you Henry". "No mother or sister Colleen"?

"Not this time Henry, it is time Jim and I spent some time together".

She smiled at him and squeezed his hand.

"I am going to ask my friend Colin, we haven't spent time together for ages"

"Colin my man how have you been keeping"? "Hello Henry, good thanks, how are you"? "I am phoning to ask if you would like two weeks in the USA, one week in New York and one in Miami, traveling by private jet, with my compliments". "I would love to H but I have a small problem".

"Which is"? "I met a girl, and we are going steady". "So where is the problem, ask her to join us, err will it be one room or two"?

"One of course old friend, we live in the 21st century or hadn't you noticed"?

They all met at the airport "This is our pilot Greg, please say hello to Colin and Isobel". They boarded the Gulf Stream, the flight began.

Henry looked at Colin, whom he met at University he was two years older, which made his age to be 44. The lady next to him, Isobel, looked to be mid thirties he guessed, she was an Architect he was informed.

They looked up and both caught his eye, they smiled, he returned the smile but feeling sheepish for some reason, he switched on the computer.

A different driver was waiting at the airport and they arrived at the same hotel, near Central Park.

Both couples, obviously wanting to be alone with their partners, excused them selves for dinner and went off in separate taxis.

Henry took a table to seat two people near the window and looked out at the view, after glancing at the menu, and deciding what he would have, he looked casually around the large, opulent dining room.

His fellow diners were mainly elderly couples, most had tables for four.

There was a very attractive lady wearing a red suit, with black hair, studying the menu, she looked up and caught his gaze, both looked away in embarrassment. The waiter arrived, took his order, and brought him a bottle of his favourite red wine. Loosening his tie a little, he took a sip of wine, his eyes were drawn back to the lady, who had been looking at him, and she immediately looked away.

He smiled "This is ridiculous" raising his hand he called the waiter "please bring me pen and paper".

He wrote "Hello my name is Henry, and I would like to invite you to join me for dinner, or I will join you if you prefer. No strings attached I promise you, good conversation and a good dinner guaranteed."

"Waiter would you take this to that lady wearing red".

She read the note, and smiled at him informing him in sign language that she would join him, the waiter carried her drink.

Rising to his feet he shook her small hand in greeting and he could not help but notice her exquisite nails "Hello, I am Helen, very nice to meet you.

Ignoring the waiter's attempt, but giving him a large smile of thanks, he held the chair for her to sit "Oh a true gentleman at last" she smiled.

"So Helen, it is necessary for us both to go through the old ritual of finding out about each other, so I will start" he smiled. I live in England; I am a banker by profession but currently dabbling in other things. I am divorced, totally and cleanly, my ex wife now lives in France". He continued "I have no children, my parents have both passed away, and if is the correct thing to say in this day and age, I am 42". "Oh sorry" he added I am staying in this hotel for a week, then to Miami for a further week".

"I must say that is refreshingly honest, I will try to follow you" she smiled, her teeth were white, and she had the most gorgeous blue eyes he noticed.

I live in Boston, am here for three days, and run a small travel agency, my parents live four miles away from me, and I love them both dearly. I have an elder sister, I refuse to tell you my age but I am five years younger than you.

My divorced happened six years ago, also no children, did I miss anything out"? She offered her smile, which stirred Henry deep in his groin.

"The waiter has been so good" he remarked, "he waited until we made our introductions, I swear, before taking our order, here he comes now".

He order the lobster and encouraged her to do the same, he could not know it, but she was ready to order the same when sat alone, she adored lobster.

"What would you like to drink my dear", he asked. "Can I have a taste of your wine"? "Oh yes, that is wonderful". She said.

They enjoyed a wonderful evening together, both chatted honestly, without any signs of pretence, and found that they shared many opinions.

It was still early and Henry asked "Would you care for a tour of New York, I have only been here once, for two days of business.

"I would love to Henry, will you give me ten minutes to change it could be a little chilly outside". "Certainly Helen, I should put on an overcoat also".

The doorman hailed a taxi; Henry slipped him a ten dollar bill, and held the door for her to enter, he saw a small flash of white thigh as she wriggled herself into the other seat. "Where to Buddy"? "Will you please take us on a slow tour of your beautiful city, and point out all the special attractions".

"Can I check with my boss, that it is ok, I am supposed to run a set route".

Speaking on his short wave radio "Yo Herbie, dis is Benny speakin, I ave a customer who wants a full tour of de Big Apple, is it ok wid j yer"?

"Naw it aint Benny, I ave no one else to cover Time Square". "Get someone else ya fat bum or drive yerself, I got me two gen you ine customer who want der full event. I am yo best f—g driver anyways". "Seein as ya puts it so nicely Benny, go head". "I love New York humour" the banker whispered to his delightful companion.

The cabbie gave the couple a wonderful tour of New Work, even stopping in the Bronx for them to enjoy a pizza at one of Benny's cousin's pizzeria.

Pulling up outside the hotel three hours after leaving, Benny said a little sheepishly "six hundred and fifty three dollars on the clock Mack".

Henry gave him a thousand dollars and whispered "You are definitely the best cabbie in the Big Apple Benny". "Tanks chief" he replied, itching to get home to his Rosie, to tell her what a tip he had just received.

"Thank you for a wonderful evening Helen, may I see you tomorrow".

"In the evening yes Henry, but I have to attend a travel seminar in the day, we start at 10am. I would duck it, but they paid for the trip".

"I have nothing else to do, may I join you, it could be interesting".

"I will see you for breakfast at 8 am". "You have a deal my dear" said the ex banker, taking her hand and kissing it lightly.

"Gosh he makes my toes curl, he is such a gentleman, and not bad looking". She said riding in the lift to her single room.

"She is a beautiful woman, I could spend the rest of my life just looking at her face" he said "She is so gracious, and enjoys everything", he said riding in the lift to his private suite.

Henry was down to breakfast early, Jim and Colleen greeted him, "we missed you last night, did you have a good evening". "I had a wonderful evening thank you, excuse me here she comes now".

"Good morning Helen, did you sleep well"? "Yes thank you".

"Helen may I introduce my friends Jim and Colleen".

"Are you ready my dear" he said, after they had finished breakfast, and turning to his friends he said "We are off to attend a Travel Seminar, will see you later".

"Good for him" said Colleen, "it is about time he found someone else, he is such a lovely man, and she is gorgeous".

Colin and Isobel never appeared for breakfast, so the invisible man and his faithful wife climbed into a taxi and went to see the Statue of Liberty.

The Seminar was held in the top floor of a large travel agency in downtown Manhatton. Henry was not able to participate, so he sat at the back.

He smiled at Helen every time she looked in his direction, which was quite often, she tried her best to be attentive, but it was difficult for her.

"Henry I am so sorry it is a working lunch, I'm afraid you will have to pop outside and grab a sandwich, do you mind".

"For you senorita I killa da bull" he said gallantly, bowing like a Matador.

"Oh I could eat him" said the Bostonian lady.

The Seminar ended and they took a walk together, he was thrilled when she put her arm through his and they strolled together down a long wooded road.

"Arriving back at the hotel, Henry had decided that he had found the woman that he intended to spend the rest of his days with, he needed to know if she felt the same as he did, because there was no way he would allow her to slip away from his grasp.

He remembered the name of the Italian Restaurant that the yellow taxi cab had taken on the previous visit, that would do nicely he thought.

"Cabbie do you know where Dino's restaurant is"?

"Mister, every cabbie in New York knows where Dino's is, the best Italian food in the Big Apple"

"Seated in the homely restaurant with the smell of baking pizza, roasting garlic and the unmistakable aroma of a wood burning oven, he took both of Helens hands in his "Helen I haven't known you for long, but still long enough to know that you are the one for me. I will court you in the proper way that pleases you and your parents, but I want to be honest with you.

I am rich, I have my own plane, I would like to fly you back to Boston when you leave, I want to see you every week end, if you want me to".

"Henry, I am not a dumb 16 year old anymore I know what I want and I am sure that I have found it, I say yes to everything". She said, her eyes shining.

Wanting to invite him to stay with her tonight, but only staying in a tiny room with a single bed, they would wait for the right time.

Later at her bedroom door they kissed goodnight, passionately on the lips, their tongues touching each other, and both of them understood why they would not make love tonight, but it would keep.

"My god Henry is this really yours' she said, gazing round the inside of the Gulf Stream in awe. "It is my dear, and I have a Rolls Royce as well", but nobody to share them with Helen, I hope it will be you my love".

"I hope so to my darling, I have waited all my life for you".

"So my invisible friend, you and I have come a long way since you put that bloody piano wire round my neck and almost killed me".

"I plead guilty your honour, but I also think I knocked some bloody sense into you, you used to raid old peoples pension funds before I met you"

"I cannot deny it" said the ex banker, "but I am reformed".

"Jim I need to ask if you, are you now satisfied with your passion to rid the world of baddies, you turned an African country into one of the happiest on the planet by getting rid of a despot leader, you put thirteen drug dealers in jail for selling drugs to children, you single handedly closed thirty six premises that manufactured and sold drugs, you gave over two million to police widows and Orphans, and finally you converted the hardest drug barons on the planet into one of the most generous and hardworking men, helping to fight drugs.

You should be knighted Jim but nobody knows your identity.

I think god is now happy with what you have done, and I as your friend salute you", and finally my friend I see every day how you and Colleen love each other, is it worth losing your life to take on one of those evil Eastern European people smugglers, I think that is not fair to Colleen".

"Yes you are right Henry, I think it is time for Colleen and me to buy that villa in Spain, and enjoy our lives, will you come and visit"?

Most of my time will be spent in America with Helen, but when can get to Spain, of course we will call and see you".

"Goodbye my invisible assassin, it was good to know you, and I am honoured to be called your friend".

ABOUT THE AUTHOR

I WAS BORN IN BRADFORD, Yorkshire in 1939, educated to grammar school level, quite good at sports, representing Bradford at football and cricket. Served an apprenticeship as a draughtsman, and then moved to estimating. Spent 2 years in Australia and 28 years in South Africa, returning to England in 2010 where I live with my wife Elena.

Having just retired and not knowing how to fill the days, she persuaded me to write my first book my life story 'Jam Tomorrer'

If you believe the myth of Pegasus the horse with wings who gives one ideas and inspiration, then he has sat on my shoulder ever since as I wrote another book called 'The Pure Magic of True Love', followed by nine short stories for children.

Seth the Salt Pot, Roger the Red Engine, Sid the Swallow, Melvin the Mouse, Benny the Beaver, Greg the Greyhound, Denis the Duck, Cedric the Salmon and Ernie the Elephant are my small adventure stories.

My latest book called The Invisible Assassin has now been published, and I am in the process of writing another one of the same character.

My wife and I enjoy visiting castles and museums; we love history, nature and animals, and when we are able, travel in Europe.

I am into any sport played with a ball, and a Chelsea supporter of long standing.

I enjoy reading, Wilbur Smith and Robert Ludlum are my favourite authors but if I pick up a book that I like, I will read until it is finished.

I have a son and two grandchildren in England, and a daughter in South Africa.

Elena has a daughter in Russia.

Lightning Source UK Ltd.
Milton Keynes UK
UKOW041559190413

209502UK00001B/104/P